WHY THE WAR WAS WRONG

WHY THE WAR WAS WRONG

Edited by RAIMOND GAITA

With contributions by
**ROBERT MANNE, GUY RUNDLE, EVA SALLIS,
RAIMOND GAITA, HILARY CHARLESWORTH,
PETER COGHLAN, MARK MCKENNA**

TEXT PUBLISHING MELBOURNE AUSTRALIA

The Text Publishing Company
171 La Trobe Street
Melbourne Victoria 3000
Australia
www.textpublishing.com.au

First published in 2003 by The Text Publishing Company

Designed by Mr Chong
Typeset in 11.7/16 Bembo by J&M Typesetting
Printed by Griffin Press

National Library of Australia Cataloguing-in-Publication data:

Why the war was wrong.
ISBN 1 920885 12 9.
1. Iraq War, 2003. I. Gaita, Raimond, 1946- .

956.70443

CONTENTS

THE CONTRIBUTORS

Hilary Charlesworth is Professor of International Law and Director of the Centre for International and Public Law in the Faculty of Law, Australian National University.

Peter Coghlan is a Senior Lecturer in the School of Philosophy, Australian Catholic University, Melbourne. He has published papers and articles in the fields of Ethics, Aesthetics and Philosophy of Religion. He is an active contributor in magazines, journals and the daily press to public debate on significant moral issues of the day.

Raimond Gaita is Professor of Moral Philosophy, Kings College, University of London and Professor of Philosophy at the Australian Catholic University. His books include the award-winning *Romulus, My Father, Good and Evil: An Absolute Conception, A Common Humanity: Thinking About Love & Truth & Justice* and *The Philosopher's Dog.*

Robert Manne is Professor of Politics at La Trobe University and a columnist for the *Age* and the *Sydney Morning Herald*. His books include *The Culture of Forgetting, The Way We Live Now, The Australian Century, In Denial, The Barren Years* and *Whitewash.*

Mark McKenna is an Australian Research Council Fellow in History at the Australian National University in Canberra. His most recent book *Looking for Blackfellas' Point: An Australian*

History of Place (UNSW Press 2002) won the Douglas Stewart Prize for Non-Fiction and the Book of the Year in the 2003 NSW Premier's Literary Awards.

Guy Rundle is a co-editor of *Arena Magazine*, and a writer and producer for television and stage. His most recent works include the Max Gillies stage show *Your Dreaming*, and *The Opportunist: John Howard and the Triumph of Reaction* (Black Inc).

Eva Sallis is an Australian-born writer. Her first novel *Hiam* won the *Australian* Vogel and the Dobbie literary awards. Her most recent novels are *The City of Sealions* and *Mahjar* and she has co-edited a number of anthologies, including *Dark Dreams: Australian Refugee Stories*, due out early in 2004. She is co-founder and current president of Australians Against Racism Inc. She travels regularly to the Middle East.

Earlier versions of the contributions by Peter Coghlan, Hilary Charlesworth, Raimond Gaita, Robert Manne and Guy Rundle were public lectures in the series 'The Invasion of Iraq', sponsored by the School of Philosophy, Australian Catholic University and held at the university's St Patrick's Campus, Fitzroy, in July and August 2003.

Part of Raimond Gaita's essay was first published in the May 2003 issue of *Australian Book Review.*

INTRODUCTION

We invaded Iraq to disarm Saddam Hussein of weapons of mass destruction with which terrorists were likely to attack us. So George W. Bush, Tony Blair and John Howard told us. The 'coalition of the willing' killed ten of thousands of Iraqis, put at risk the lives of its soldiers, undermined international law and the institutions that support it and embarked on a political adventure whose consequences no one can soberly predict, in one of the most volatile parts of the world. Yet five months after President Bush declared the war won, neither weapons of mass destruction nor evidence of programs to build them have been found.

It is still too early to know with what mixture of innocent ignorance, culpable ignorance, self-deception, distortion of intelligence documents and outright lies the leaders of the coalition presented their case. It has been evident for some months that they did not know what they claimed to know. Now, after the Iraq Survey Group's interim report and the publication of the diary of former British foreign secretary Robin Cook, the situation is even clearer: it seems highly unlikely they had serious reason to believe that Saddam posed a grave enough threat for them to deny UN chief weapons inspector Hans Blix the extra time for which he pleaded. Incredibly, they still ask their citizens to trust them. The mendacious histories of their governments deprive them of the right to do it.

Discontent with the occupation grows daily in the US, but only the British are holding their head of government to account for the right reason—because the arguments were weak from the beginning and are now almost entirely bereft of factual support. Tony Blair, it is true, is totally unrepentant. Indeed he alone amongst the leaders of the coalition declines to act as though the liberation of the Iraqis was always the real purpose of the war. For a mixture of good and bad reasons the disenchantment with him that has descended on almost 70 per cent of the British electorate will probably not cost him the leadership of his party nor Labour the next election. It is likely, however, to ensure that Britain will not soon go to war again for the kind of reasons he gave. The British people have refused to put behind them an examination of why they went to war, or to succumb to the moral bullying that denigrates such questioning as a self-indulgent and divisive distraction from the urgent task of rebuilding Iraq. Their resistance puts Australia to shame.

None of the contributors to this book gloats over the fact that no weapons of mass destruction or programs to build them have been found. We did not oppose the war because we assumed that Saddam did not have such weapons. Certainly, the continuing American, British and Iraqi casualties give us no pleasure. Nor does the fact that politically things appear to be going badly and will almost certainly get worse before they get better, if they get better. Were US dreams of 'planting democracy' in Iraq to come true we would rejoice, for Iraq and for the possibilities in the region. We are not blind to Saddam's brutality, nor do we underestimate the great difference that exists between the democratic governments of the coalition (despite erosions of civil liberties since September 11) and the brutal regimes that the kind of terrorists who piloted the planes into the twin towers would wish to impose on those whom they had not first eliminated as vermin.

All of us are glad that Saddam's criminal government has fallen and we hope that he will be captured and brought to trial, preferably in an international court. None of us believes that the war was a just means to those achievements.

Understandably our government is keen to divert attention from the fact that through the agency of the armed forces of the coalition we killed tens of thousands of Iraqis. Liberated Iraq is presented for our contemplation, abstracted from the human cost of its achievement, in the hope that we will celebrate its benefits without much unease, ambiguous though the benefits now seem. And when dead Iraqis do press on our conscience, we are invited to effect another abstraction—to assess, independently of our agency in the matter, whether the benefits are worth the cost.

These kinds of abstractions seek to evade the moral reality that the dead are the most important cost of the war and that most of them are dead because we and our allies killed them. To resist such evasion is one of the foremost reasons why the essays in this book were assembled. Intellectuals, journalists and politicians who become intoxicated by the grand projects of geopolitics often affect an urbane worldliness that disposes them to condescend to serious protest over the fact that they are prepared to sacrifice countless thousands of human beings to those projects. They, especially, must ask themselves who they think they are, with what right they have taken it upon themselves to rearrange the world according to their dreams. But they should not take that question as being in the first instance a challenge from their fellow citizens. With all the sobriety they can they can muster, they should imagine it as put to them by those we maimed, by those whose lives we shattered and by those who grieve for the men, women and children we killed.

Writing in the *New York Times*, Thomas Friedman distinguished three kinds of reasons we should consider when we reflect on our attitude to the war. First, there are the reasons given by the coalition. Secondly, there are the reasons that actually motivated it to go to war—the 'real reasons' Friedman called them. Thirdly, there is the 'right reason'. He believed it was the intention to liberate the Iraqis from Saddam's brutal oppression. He and others who drew much the same distinctions argued that the third reason (it came to be called the 'humanitarian' case) was of itself enough to justify invading Iraq, though none of the leaders of the coalition had put it as a reason and though Howard and Blair denied it could be a sufficient reason.

In this book that case is rejected, but I do not think anyone could fairly say that it is not treated seriously. It is rejected on its own terms and because to regard it as justification for a war fought for other reasons is to accord insufficient weight to the fact that, in a democracy, the reasons politicians give for going to war, the reasons why they actually go and the reasons which would justify going should all ideally coincide. Realistically, of course, they often do not; but only in extreme circumstances (intervening to prevent genocide of the kind that occurred in Rwanda, for example) can the right reason for waging war be one that the electorate would not have accepted. And if the reasons given publicly are seriously discrepant from the 'real' reasons, then the public might become not only cynical but justifiably angry about having been treated with contempt.

To those who welcomed the war because they saw in it a moral opportunity to do what they believed should have been done long before, we urge acknowledgment of the costs to democracy of such 'opportunism'. It is one thing to believe that it would have been right to invade Iraq if the electorate had been convinced of the humanitarian case. It is another thing to believe it was right to invade though it was not. The difference puts extreme pressure on the comforting thought that we did what is right even if we did it for the wrong reasons.

On Anzac Day some years ago I heard on the radio, in the words of a British poet, a beautiful elegy to Australian soldiers who had fallen in the two world wars. I knew the praise to be truthful because I recognised the qualities the poet celebrated in the men (and in many of the women) I had known in my childhood in country Victoria. An anecdote by one of the Dunera boys—German Jewish men who fled to Britain from Nazi Germany, were arrested as enemy aliens and then shipped on SS *Dunera* to detention camps in Australia—shows what the qualities are. He was at the back of the column as it marched to a camp on the fringes of the desert. The Australian soldier guarding him stopped, handed him his rifle and said, 'Here mate. Hold this while I go to have a piss.' The Dunera boy said that he knew then that he was in heaven.

John Howard believes he speaks for Australians whose love of country and sense of national identity were partly formed by acquaintance with and admiration for such men.

But I see nothing of that soldier's straightness in Howard's mendacity; nothing of his egalitarianism in Howard's contempt for the electorate; nothing of his modesty in Howard's hubris when, intoxicated by the prestige of his friendship with the president of the world's only superpower, he lectured the UN, the Germans and the French for being derelict in the exercise of their responsibilities. Especially wonderful was the guileless simplicity with which the soldier acknowledged his common humanity with his prisoner. How different things might have been if that soldier's spirit had graced our politics.

Raimond Gaita
London, September 29, 2003

EXPLAINING THE INVASION

Robert Manne

I

In March 2003, the United States and Great Britain, with the support of Australia, invaded, conquered and then occupied Iraq. The argument for the invasion was mounted by the leaders of the anglophone democracies on the basis of the danger Iraq posed both to its Middle Eastern neighbours—especially to Kuwait and Israel—and to the west. According to these leaders Iraq was known to possess a vast arsenal of weapons of mass destruction, which were ready to be deployed in war. According to these leaders Iraq, in addition, was known to have an active program for the development of nuclear weapons which was, at most, a few years from success. The danger Iraq posed to its neighbours was assumed to come from its willingness to use its weapons in an unanticipated strike. The danger it was said to pose to the west was either through clandestine passage of weapons of mass destruction to terrorist groups or through the use of nuclear blackmail to achieve its ends.

At present there are two main questions concerning the invasion of Iraq. Was it lawful or just? How is the invasion to be explained? I am concerned with both questions in this essay, but in particular with the second. My attempt to find an explanation for the invasion is not driven by mere intellectual curiosity. A true explanation, if it can be discovered, will provide vital clues as to the likely character of the coming age.

II

Any attempt at an explanation of the invasion of Iraq must begin, in my opinion, not with oil but with ideology, with the influence of neoconservatism, the most powerful ideological stream in American political life at the present time.

Neoconservatism has three interconnected main themes. In its social dimension it is hostile to the progressivism of the 1960s and 1970s, to positive racial discrimination and the redistributive activities of the modern welfare state. One of the godfathers of neoconservatism, Irving Kristol, once famously defined the tribe as comprising liberals who had been mugged by reality. Neoconservatism's favourite piece of social science is the law of unintended consequences. The *locus classicus* of this dimension of neoconservatism is Charles Murray's study of the perverse effects of social welfare, *Losing Ground*.

In its cultural dimension neoconservatism defends the moral and literary values of western civilisation from the antinomian revolution waged, since the sixties, by relativists, postmodernists, multiculturalists, feminists and the custodians of political correctness. The *locus classicus* here is Allan Bloom's *The Closing of the American Mind*, behind which can be found the influence of the Jewish German political philosopher Leo Strauss, the founder of an academic cult which played a part in the intellectual formulation of several of the most influential neoconservatives.

In its defence and foreign policy dimension, neoconservatism once represented the attempt to revive the spirit of anti-communism, after the battering it had taken during the Vietnam War. During this period its most important American publicist was Norman Podhoretz, the editor of *Commentary* magazine. In its present incarnation neoconservative foreign policy thought is dominated by strategies aimed at capitalising on the American victory in the Cold War and the arrival of the post-Cold War era of American global hegemony. Presently the most prominent publicist for the defence and foreign policy dimension of neoconservatism is William Kristol, the son of Irving and editor of the Murdoch-financed *Weekly Standard*.

The first genuinely influential neoconservatives who moved from magazines or academia into mainstream politics were Richard Perle and Paul Wolfowitz, both postgraduate students of the University of Chicago nuclear-weapons strategist and *über*-hawk, Albert Wohlstetter. During the 1970s Perle and Wolfowitz worked on the staff of the Democrat Henry 'Scoop' Jackson, an anti-Kissinger, anti-détentiste, anti-Soviet Cold Warrior. During the 1980s they and several other prominent neocons joined the Reagan administration and became enthusiasts for his muscular, internationalist brand of defence and foreign policy. During the 1990s, now in exile during the Clinton years, the neocons regrouped. Many were founding members of the Project for the New American Century, an offshoot of the most powerful neoconservative think-tank, the American Enterprise Institute.

Nineties foreign policy neoconservatism argued against the status quo 'realism' of both Henry Kissinger and the first President Bush. Its advocates called, instead, for what William Kristol in a 1996 article in *Foreign Affairs* described as a 'neo-Reaganite foreign policy of military supremacy and moral confidence'. The neocons were witheringly critical of the directionlessness of foreign policy under Clinton, whom they claimed was squandering the splendid opportunities opened by the American victory in the Cold War and the new era of US global hegemony. They wanted to combine Woodrow Wilson's interest in spreading the American ideals of liberal democracy and free markets with Theodore Roosevelt's instinctive understanding of the uses of military power.

Despite the fact that the US had no serious major enemy, the neocons advocated a heavy increase in US defence spending of something in the order of an additional $80 billion per annum. They also supported a military strategy, first outlined by Defense Secretary Dick Cheney and his under-secretary Paul Wolfowitz in the dying days of the Bush Senior administration, which aimed at ensuring permanent American military superiority over all possible rivals. The neocons were worried about the eventual challenge of China. In his 1996 *Foreign Affairs* article, William Kristol even wrote of a China policy looking ultimately towards 'regime change' there. For the neocons the oceans barely reached to their knees.

The neoconservatives were also preoccupied by the Middle East. All were not merely uncritical and unconditional supporters of Israel, but also well connected to the most hawkish element of Likud. Many were hostile to Clinton's attempts to broker peace between Israel and the Palestinians. Many were enthusiasts for and had learned from the Israeli idea of the pre-emptive military strike, as seen, for example, in the Israeli decision to take out the Iraqi nuclear facility at Osirak in 1981. All were extremely hostile to Israel's enemies in the Middle East—Iran, Syria and, above all, Iraq.

This is of critical importance. Well before September 11 the neocons advocated the end of the Iraqi regime. One of the early initiatives of the Program for the New American

Century was an open letter to President Clinton in January 1998 signed by eighteen prominent neoconservatives, including Donald Rumsfeld, Richard Perle, Paul Wolfowitz, Douglas Feith and William Kristol, which called for the armed overthrow of Saddam Hussein. Of all the neocons, however, the most serious advocate of a strategy to achieve this end was Paul Wolfowitz, who presented to the House National Security Committee in September 1998 a plan for providing arms and money to Ahmad Chalabi's Iraqi National Congress, the Iraqi émigré organisation especially favoured by the neocons. He also argued for the creation of an anti-Saddam military enclave in the oil-rich, Shia-dominated south, under American military protection, a parallel to the Kurdish enclave already established in the north. The purpose of the southern enclave was to attract disloyal elements of the Iraqi army and, eventually, to engineer the unravelling of the regime.

In the lead-up to the November 2000 presidential election, the loyalties of the PNAC neocons were divided between Republican contenders Senator John McCain and Governor George W. Bush. Indeed, during the campaign Bush made certain noises about the unwisdom of American involvement in 'nation building' and the dangers of American 'hubris' which were unpleasing to the neocons and which smelt to them of old conservative 'isolationism'. Despite these misgivings, however, what turned out to be of far greater significance for the neocons was Bush's choice of Dick

Cheney as his vice-presidential running mate. Cheney was a founding member of PNAC. Largely due to his influence, following the election of Bush, many of the most prominent neocons—including ten of the eighteen signatories of the letter to Clinton on Iraq—moved into critical positions in the new administration. John Bolton and Richard Armitage took senior posts in the Department of State. Donald Rumsfeld, Paul Wolfowitz and Douglas Feith occupied the three most senior jobs in the Department of Defense.

There was little evidence that in the first months of 2001 the neocons were making serious policy headway. Differences appeared between the neocons inside and outside government, with the *Weekly Standard* criticising the administration for being 'soft' on China and Russia and insufficiently pro-Israel. Perhaps the neocons expected to be disappointed by any administration. Before the 2000 election the PNAC had produced an extraordinary imperial plan for a new global Pax Americana, in a paper called *Rebuilding America's Defenses*. In this paper they argued that the shift to the more aggressive global strategy they desired would happen only gradually, unless there were to be 'some catastrophic and catalysing event, like a new Pearl Harbor'.

As it happened, this was a prescient remark, providing food for several conspiracy theorists in the future. September 11 presented the neocons, situated at the heart of the US government, with their historic chance.

III

Following September 11 the Bush administration, in coalition with a number of countries, including Britain and Australia, went to war against Afghanistan after the Taliban, as anticipated, failed to hand over the al Qaeda military forces based on their territory. The US-led war against Afghanistan did not, in particular, reflect the influence of the neoconservatives in the Bush administration. No matter who was in the White House on September 11 it seems certain that the United States would have taken military action against al Qaeda and the regime which offered it protection and support. Given that al Qaeda had just launched an unprovoked terrorist strike on the United States, killing 3000 of its people, military action against it and its protector regime was both inevitable and just, according to the most traditional understanding of any nation's right to act in self-defence.

As is now clear, what was most important from the neoconservatives' point of view was whether or not they would be able to utilise the September 11 attack to draw the Bush presidency towards the kind of defence and foreign policy position they had been advocating in more tranquil times.

The most influential neocons out of government interpreted September 11 in genuinely apocalyptic terms. Michael Ledeen called for a 'total war' against America's enemies. Eliot

A. Cohen spoke of the beginning of the Fourth World War (the Third had been the Cold War) between western civilisation and radical Islam. Norman Podhoretz argued that, as a result of the arrival of this new world war, the United States might soon find itself 'forced...to topple five or six or seven more tyrannies in the Islamic world.' He also nicely captured the metamorphosis that had occurred in the spirit of the US President in the months following September 11. 'One hears that Bush,' he wrote in *Commentary* in February 2002, 'who entered the White House without a clear sense of what he wanted to do there, now feels that there was a purpose behind his election all along; as a born-again Christian, it is said, he believes he was chosen by God to eradicate the evil of terrorism from the world. I think it is a plausible rumour.'

At the time of September 11 the neocons in the Bush administration were the only group with a clear foreign policy vision that answered to the President's needs and reflected his new mood. The intellectual and policy work they had now to do was to translate the war on terror, which had begun with al Qaeda and Afghanistan, into the first instalment of their plans for the grand policy transformation of which they dreamed. With Bush's State of the Union address in January 2002, where the President announced the existence of an 'axis of evil' of Iraq, Iran and North Korea, their victory for the mind of the President was becoming clear. Before a hearing of the Senate Foreign Relations Committee on 7 February 2002, William Kristol outlined the scope and nature of that victory with admirable clarity.

At first, Kristol argued, Bush had declared war on al Qaeda; then he had declared war on all terrorists who possessed what he called 'global reach', that is a capacity to trouble the United States. By November, having grasped the danger posed by terrorists armed with nuclear, chemical or biological weapons, he had turned his attention, finally, from 'terrorist groups to terror-loving states'. Kristol continued:

> The State of the Union address marked the maturation of the Bush doctrine. This war, according to the President, has 'two great objectives'. The first is defeating terrorism. The second objective, marking the most significant declaration by an American president in almost 20 years, is an unequivocal rejection of the international status quo. 'The United States of America,' said President Bush, 'will not permit the world's most dangerous regimes to threaten us with the world's most destructive weapons.'
>
> And President Bush singled out three regimes, North Korea, Iran and Iraq, as enemies; they constitute an 'axis of evil' that poses 'a grave and growing danger'. Nor will he 'stand by, as peril draws closer and closer'. Time, he said, 'is not on our side'. The President is thus willing to act

pre-emptively, and, if need be, unilaterally. This is a matter of American self-defense.

Nor was this all the Bush doctrine implied. As Kristol pointed out, the President was concerned not merely with the dangers of terror regimes but also 'seeks to challenge tyranny in general'. 'No nation is exempt,' the President argued, from the 'true and unchanging' American principles of justice and liberty.

Kristol was asked by the senators a more practical question. 'What's next in the war on terrorism?' For the neocons inside and outside the Bush administration he answered with a single word—'Iraq'. The war on terrorism had, then, according to Kristol, by the time of President Bush's January 2002 State of the Union address, already been transformed into a revolutionary strategy for Pax Americana, on a global scale. Reaction to September 11 had begun to reshape American foreign policy according to the neocons' desires. The war on terrorism would extend, naturally, to war against Iraq.

IV

Four years separated the first articulation of the Containment Doctrine by George Kennan, at the origin of the Cold War, from its ultimate crystallisation in the April 1950 United

States strategic doctrine, NSC 68. By contrast, it took only nine months from Bush's State of the Union address to the final formulation of a US general doctrine for the post-September 11 world.

This new strategic doctrine argued that in the ten years following the Soviet collapse the United States had failed to grasp the nature of the threats posed by the post-Cold War world. With September 11 the US awoke. The new threats concerned not only the 'terrorists with a global range', but also what were called 'rogue states', those states which brutalised their own people, hated the United States and sought to acquire weapons of mass destruction. Although such states were less militarily formidable than the old Cold War enemy, the Soviet Union, they posed to the United States, it was argued, an even greater threat.

Why? Unlike the Soviet Union, rogue states were not 'risk averse'. For them weapons of mass destruction were weapons of choice. Rogue states believed that by using such weapons they could overcome 'the conventional military superiority' of the United States. Even worse, such states were sponsors of 'world terrorism'. Because of the 'overlap' between rogue states and global terrorist networks, the US had no alternative but to act.

We are now at the heart of the new Strategic Doctrine. The United States, it was claimed, faced the prospect of an attack either from one of the rogue states or from a terrorist group supplied by them with weapons of mass destruction. In the face of this kind of threat Cold War ideas about deterrence and containment were obsolete. The only rational military strategy was the so-called 'pre-emptive strike'.

According to the Bush doctrine, the idea of the pre-emptive strike as a legitimate form of self-defence could be found in the mainstream tradition of international law. In this tradition, the use of a pre-emptive strike is justified at a time when enemy forces are massing; that, is when a 'visible' threat appears. After September 11, however, circumstances changed. The new enemy was invisible. It might strike with lethal weapons without warning at any time. 'Even if uncertainty remains as to the time and place of the enemy attack', under the new Bush doctrine the United States claimed the right to mount pre-emptive strikes.

There were two glaring flaws in this new doctrine. The first involved the mis-characterisation of the likely behaviour of the enemy. Or, to put it more precisely: concerning the likely behaviour of the enemy, the doctrine was half-wrong and half-right. It is almost self-evident, at least to me, that if one of the Islamist terrorist networks linked to al Qaeda were ever to become equipped with weapons of mass destruction, they would do everything within their power to use these weapons against the civilian population of the United States. They are driven by a pure hatred of Americans and Jews. The organisations have, even more importantly, nothing to lose other than their operatives' lives. This half of the doctrine makes sense.

Where it collapses is in its view of the likely behaviour of the rogue state. According to the Bush doctrine, such states are amassing weapons of mass destruction for the purpose of launching attacks against the United States, either directly or through proxy terrorist groups. For such an assumption neither evidence nor logic exists. The doctrine implied not merely that the leaders of the rogue states were extremely brutal (which was true) but also that they were, effectively, suicidal madmen who were willing to allow their regimes to be destroyed through the fleeting pleasure derived from inflicting lethal damage on the object of their hatred, the United States. There was nothing in the history of either Saddam Hussein's Iraq or communist North Korea which indicated that insane behaviour of this kind—of a surprise attack or collusion with a terrorist group (which would be open to detection)—was even remotely likely to occur.

Yet more needs to be said than this. Because the doctrine proposed military action against rogue states when no threat to the US was imminent, what was really being proposed was a strategy not of pre-emptive strike but of preventive war, a strategy that the US military planners in NSC 68, at the most hawkish moment of the Cold War, described as 'unthinkable' and 'repugnant' to civilised opinion. For a preventive war to be launched, according to this new doctrine, a state need only imagine itself, at some time in the future, to be under threat. With such an idea the line between self-defence and aggression had become hopelessly blurred.

The danger of this conflation of the pre-emptive strike and preventive war was aggravated precisely by the fact that the Bush doctrine made it clear that the US reserved for itself the right to strike unilaterally without mandate from the established procedures of the United Nations. Under the new doctrine, then, the US not only reserved for itself the right to go to war on the basis of an imagined threat. It also arrogated to itself the exclusive right to decide when and where such a threat existed.

At the centre of the doctrine a great conceptual hole was present. Did the US alone possess the sovereign right to act unilaterally against a supposed threat to its security by prosecuting a preventive war, or did an identical right exist for other states? If all states possessed this right, the Bush doctrine opened the way for a return to the law of the jungle, where the powerful have the capacity to impose their will on the weak.

If, on the other hand, the right did not exist for other states, the Bush doctrine amounted to an almost formal claim to US world hegemony. That is what the neocons proposed. And that was what, I believe, the new doctrine claimed. This was the doctrine for the new era of US global hegemony.

V

There is considerable direct and circumstantial evidence that, by the time of the enunciation of the revolutionary new US strategic doctrine, the American and British governments had already decided upon the invasion of Iraq. It was also certain by now that if the United States and Britain went to war against Iraq Australia would come along.

There are a number of plausible reasons why, among the several possible rogue state candidates for invasion, the choice fell on Iraq. Since 1991 for the neocons and others Iraq remained unfinished business. The failure of the first Bush administration to march on Baghdad was viewed as a humiliation and as a mistake. Some neocons probably also genuinely regretted the terrible betrayal of the Shias, who were encouraged to rebel after Saddam had been driven out of Kuwait. Because, moreover, of the various ambiguities surrounding the disarmament provisions of the 1991 peace settlement and the withdrawal of the UN inspectors in 1998, there existed a thin legal case to legitimise the invasion of Iraq which did not exist in the cases of North Korea or Iran. In addition the neocons believed a Middle East peace was possible without serious concessions needing to be made by the Israelis. They were tempted by the strange thought that the road to peace between the Israelis and Palestinians passed through Baghdad.

For all I know some senior members of both the Bush and Blair governments might have genuinely feared that Iraq might launch an attack on one of its neighbours or even pass lethal weapons to al Qaeda. For all I know even Bush and Blair might have believed such a thing—Bush because of his moderate intelligence and Blair because of his self-infatuation, which led him to the idea that in the end almost anything he said was true. What I am not convinced of is that any of the architects of the new strategy genuinely believed in the danger posed by Iraq. The neocons are many things. But they are not fools. In the build-up to the war, time and again, they expressed the true opinion that, after a decade of disarmament and sanctions, Iraq was pathetically weak (in Perle's opinion one-third of its 1991 military strength). I doubt that they seriously believed Iraq could not be contained. I am certain that they knew that while the story they circulated before the invasion—that George W. Bush was playing Winston Churchill to Saddam Hussein's Adolf Hitler—might be useful for propaganda purposes it was, for all other purposes, utterly absurd.

The genuine aim of American policy by the summer of 2002 was to overthrow the regime of Saddam Hussein. The pretended aim, however, was to bring about the disarmament of his regime. Considerable difficulty flowed from the tension between the real and the pretended aim. Not only was the planned war unjust according to all traditional understandings, because Iraq posed no clear and present danger to its neighbours, let alone to the west. Its injustice was deepened because of the way the American public, America's allies and, soon, the United Nations, were asked to support the war for reasons that were, at best, secondary, and, at worst, of a fundamentally spurious kind.

Having decided, then, in the late summer of 2002, to mount an invasion of Iraq, the critical decision facing the Bush administration was whether to go to war unilaterally, with a handful of allies—'the coalition of the willing', in the Madison Avenue slogan—or to seek beforehand the sanction of the United Nations. Dick Cheney and Donald Rumsfeld warned about the messy complications that might flow from a United Nations entanglement. The moderates in the administration, led by Colin Powell, argued for an approach to the United Nations for reasons of diplomacy and inter-national law. After a short struggle the moderates won this battle for the mind of the President, most likely because their view was shared by Tony Blair and, even more importantly, by the old Republican elite who had served under Bush the Elder—figures such as Brent Scowcroft and James Baker.

As it turned out, concerning the messiness which would flow from seeking UN authorisation, the neocons were right. The UN Security Council agreed to demand from Iraq the resumption of weapons inspections abandoned in 1998, but to leave in its own hands, and for the future, the decision as to what to do if Iraq failed to co-operate with the inspectors. When, in February 2003, the chief weapons inspector, Hans Blix, delivered a mixed but not unfavourable report concerning Iraqi co-operation, he requested more time to complete his work. The Americans and the British refused. Moreover when it became clear that the Security Council was unwilling to sanction the use of military force without further inspections, the Americans, the British and the Australians proceeded with their invasion nevertheless. The legal basis of the invasion was Security Council resolutions made in 1991. Yet in March 2003 the Security Council, the author of these resolutions, was itself unambiguously opposed to the use of force at that time. Although lawyers will argue about these matters forever, from the viewpoint of the layman and the viewpoint of common sense, the invasion of Iraq was, by now, unlawful as well as unjust. One would have to be mad to believe that in March 2003 there was no alternative to war.

VI

One consequence of the strategy of the pre-emptive strike is the extraordinary power it transfers to the intelligence services of the supposedly threatened state. There are two reasons why this is so. It is on the basis of intelligence assessments and predictions rather than external events that states now decide whether or not to go to war. Moreover as citizens are not privy to these assessments they are asked to place their trust in the intelligence services and the governments to whom they report. In the build-up to the invasion, were the governments and the intelligence services worthy of our trust?

There is no ambiguity about what we were told by the leaders of the anglophone democracies. We were told that we were in grave danger because of the weapons of mass destruction that Iraq was said to possess. On one occasion, with his characteristic subtlety, the US Secretary of Defense, Donald Rumsfeld, explained the situation like this:

> There's no debate in the world as to whether they have these weapons. There's no debate in the world as to whether they're continuing to develop and acquire them. There's no debate in the world as to whether or not he's used them. There's no debate in the world as to whether or not he's consistently threatening his neighbours with them. We all know that. A trained ape knows that.

The anglophone leaders did not merely claim to know, in general, that Iraq possessed a vast arsenal of chemical and biological weapons. They also claimed to know—one had to assume on the basis of very solid intelligence—the precise amounts of chemical and biological agents and numbers of

27

delivery systems that Iraq possessed. The public was informed, on different occasions, that Saddam Hussein had 500 tons of mustard and nerve gas; 25,000 litres of anthrax; 38,000 litres of botulinum; and 30,000 weapons by which these chemical and biological substances could be delivered. One source of this kind of detailed intelligence was said to be Saddam's son-in-law, General Hussein Kamel, who had been in charge of Iraq's weapons program before defecting (briefly) to the west.

Nor were chemical and biological weapons the whole story. Time and again the Anglo-American leaders suggested that Saddam Hussein had an ongoing nuclear weapons program which might, in a year or so, be capable of producing deliverable bombs. In a speech of August 2002, Dick Cheney put it like this: 'We now know that Saddam Hussein has resumed his efforts to acquire nuclear weapons…Many of us are convinced that Saddam will acquire nuclear weapons fairly soon. Just how soon we cannot really gauge.' For this prediction, too, convincing evidence was produced. In September 2002, Tony Blair revealed that Iraq had recently attempted to purchase weapons-grade uranium from Niger.

Nor did the danger Iraq posed rest exclusively with its weapons of mass destruction. Perhaps even more alarming was the fact that Iraq had developed close working relations with al Qaeda. The Pentagon, for example, leaked a defector's testimony to the press. It was claimed that he had trained in

Iraq with al Qaeda terrorists and had received instruction there in the use of chemical and biological weapons.

The meaning of all this was clear. Iraq posed a clear and present danger to its neighbours and to the world. Time was not on our side. In his August speech Cheney outlined the menace of Saddam Hussein like this:

> Should all his ambitions be realised the implications would be enormous for the Middle East, for the United States, and for the peace of the world. The whole range of weapons of mass destruction then would rest in the hands of a dictator who has already shown his willingness to use such weapons…Armed with an arsenal of these weapons of terror, and seated atop ten per cent of the world's oil reserves, Saddam Hussein could then be expected to seek domination of the entire Middle East, take control of a great portion of the world's energy supplies, directly threaten America's friends throughout the region, and subject the United States or any other nation to nuclear blackmail.

On the eve of the invasion, his President, fittingly enough in an address to the American Enterprise Institute, put the matter, more succinctly, like this:

> In Iraq, a dictator is building and hiding weapons that could enable him to dominate the Middle East

and intimidate the civilised world—and we will not allow it. This same tyrant has close ties to terrorist organisations and could supply them with the terrible means to strike at this country—and America will not permit it. The danger posed by Saddam Hussein…must be confronted.

During the invasion of Iraq not one of Saddam Hussein's weapons of mass destruction was used. Following the occupation of Iraq all the most promising storage sites for these weapons were inspected. Following the occupation of Iraq many of the regime's most senior generals, intelligence officers and weapons scientists were arrested and interrogated. And yet not one weapon of mass destruction was discovered.

Disturbing evidence concerning the non-discovery of the weapons has begun to appear. Andrew Wilkie of Australia's Office of National Assessments; Greg Thielmann of the US State Department's Bureau of Intelligence and Research; and an anonymous British Defence weapons specialist have all independently accused their governments of distorting or exaggerating the intelligence on Iraqi weapons with which they were supplied. A September 2002 assessment from the Pentagon's Defense Intelligence Agency has been leaked. It argued that there existed, at that time, 'no reliable information' about the production or stockpiling of chemical weapons by Iraq. It has become clear that, although the documents concerning Iraq's supposed attempts to purchase uranium from Niger were known by US intelligence as early as February 2002 to be forgeries of the crudest kind, this information was used by Tony Blair in September 2002, by George W. Bush in January 2003 and by our own prime minister in the following month.

On the question of the deliberate distortion of intelligence concerning Iraq, by far the most disturbing evidence is contained in an article in the *New Yorker* of 12 May 2003, by the investigative journalist, Seymour Hersh. Hersh has discovered that the most important sources of intelligence on weapons of mass destruction and links between Saddam Hussein's regime and al Qaeda were not the traditional agencies, the CIA and the DIA, but a small office inside the Pentagon known as the Office of Special Plans, which was established for this purpose after September 11 by Donald Rumsfeld and Paul Wolfowitz and which was run by a neoconservative ideologue and ex-Cold Warrior, Abram Shulsky.

According to Hersh the Office of Special Plans produced the kind of intelligence its masters, already determined upon war with Iraq, required. Seek and ye shall find. Hersh argues that the Office had close connections with the Iraqi National Congress and Ahmad Chalabi and privileged access to defectors supplied by them. As all students of intelligence understand, information supplied by defectors must be treated with the greatest circumspection.

Seymour Hersh claims to have discovered that the evidence of the Iraqi defector who said he had trained alongside al Qaeda operatives was fabricated, based upon deliberate mistranslations by an interpreter supplied by the Iraqi National Congress. While the fabrication was leaked, its correction never was. Hersh also claims that, despite the fact that both Bush and Cheney relied in part upon the testimony of General Hussein Kamel for their arguments about the existence of weapons of mass destruction, when Kamel was interrogated by UN officials in 1995 he told them explicitly that 'all weapons—biological, chemical, missile, nuclear—were destroyed.' The transcript of interrogation was handed to Hersh.

The invasion of Iraq was justified on the basis of the vast arsenal of weapons of mass destruction Iraq was supposed to possess. The failure to discover any such weapons points towards one of the greatest western political scandals since 1945. Whatever were the true motives of the invaders, on present evidence it appears to be the case that the justification for the invasion was a lie.

VII

I have discovered only two studies of the number of civilian casualties suffered by the Iraqis in the month or so it took for the anglophone democracies to take Baghdad. In one study a group of AP journalists visited Iraqi hospitals in the towns and cities where military operations had taken place. They found evidence in the hospital records of 3240 civilian deaths. This count did not include cases where it was unclear whether those who died were soldiers or civilians. Nor of course did this number include the civilian dead whose bodies were not taken to a hospital. In a second study, undertaken by a group which calls itself Iraq Body Count, the figures of civilian deaths recorded by the world's media were compiled. By early October 2003 this study had arrived at a minimum of 7376 civilian deaths and a maximum of 9178. This much at least is clear. Very many more civilians died during the invasion of Iraq than as a result of the terrorist attack of September 11, without which no invasion of Iraq would have taken place.

Moreover, given that the invasion of Iraq was not precipitated by any aggressive act by the Iraqi state, it is not only the civilian deaths which now weigh on the conscience of the United States, Britain and Australia. I have not seen any study, even vaguely authoritative, which tries to estimate Iraqi military deaths. Yet it is not impossible that in the invasion of Iraq tens of thousands of their soldiers died.

It would be dishonest of me if I ended at this point. The occupying troops have discovered no weapons of mass destruction. They have, however, uncovered very many mass graves. The regime that the invading armies destroyed was about as foul as any regime in the contemporary world. Experience of secret-police-drenched dictatorships like that of Saddam Hussein suggests that they are only toppled when the dictator dies in his bed, as in the cases of Stalin and Mao, or when they are overthrown in war, as in the cases of Hitler and Pol Pot.

I do not see how anyone, at the end of the invasion of Iraq, can feel at peace. Those who supported the war supported an action which originated in ideological fantasy and imperial hubris, which was justified on the basis of astonishing falsehood, and which was, according to traditional understandings, both unlawful and unjust. Yet those who opposed the invasion, as I did, cannot wriggle away from the fact that, if our opposition had been successful, the disgusting regime of Saddam Hussein would still be in power in Iraq. From this simple, unpleasant truth there is, I am afraid, no escape.

WHAT'S LAW GOT TO DO WITH THE WAR?

Hilary Charlesworth

The great wave of concern about the war in Iraq during the first few months of 2003 now seems to have crashed. It is quickly ebbing away as Iraq is absorbed into a dull murky backdrop of trouble spots we'll be careful to avoid on our travels. Although there are some ongoing concerns about neatly wrapping up the invasion, the war is rapidly receding from the public imagination.

For a short, glamorous moment, international lawyers could feel of great relevance to the debate about whether or not our country, or the world community, should be involved with a war on Iraq. We are used to being either ignored or pushed to the margins of debates about world affairs, but suddenly everyone seemed interested in our views. Although this moment has now passed, we have a lot to learn from what has happened. I want to discuss here the international law applicable to the decision to go to war, to the conduct of the hostilities, and to the situation now that the fighting is officially over.

Going to war

The debate about whether it was legal to invade Iraq was, for a while, *the* major international issue. Although George W. Bush had clearly signalled his hostility to Iraq in his famous 2002 State of the Union address, the United States and its coalition partners nevertheless thought it important to make legal arguments to justify the invasion. The United States had a complex set of legal justifications, some radical in their conception and some quite traditional, drawing on existing doctrines. Its allies in the coalition of the willing varied in their adoption of the suite of legal rationales.

The most radical and far-reaching of the justifications was announced officially in a speech by President Bush at West Point Military Academy in May 2002 and then elaborated by the National Security Council in September 2002. This was the doctrine of pre-emptive self-defence. It can be summarised as the right to use force to prevent a future attack by another state, even when there is no evidence that an attack has been planned. The argument was that Iraq, a 'rogue state', part of the 'axis of evil' which harboured aggressive intentions towards the United States, held stocks of weapons of mass destruction and constituted an ongoing threat to the United States.

For a while, Australia seemed to toy with the idea of supporting the US doctrine of pre-emptive self-defence.

The Defence Minister, Senator Robert Hill, gave some backing to the idea and in December 2002 Mr Howard said that he would like to see the UN Charter amended to allow pre-emptive action against terrorists.

There is little doubt that the doctrine is inconsistent with the UN Charter which prohibits the use of force except in two circumstances: when authorised by the UN Security Council under Chapter VII of the Charter; and in self-defence when an armed attack occurs or is imminent.

Apart from its inconsistency with the fundamental purposes of the UN Charter, it's clear also that a doctrine of pre-emptive self-defence could lead to international chaos as it provides no objective test for determining when a threat exists. The doctrine leaves the perception of threat in the eye of the country claiming the right. Ironically, the doctrine of pre-emptive self-defence would have allowed Saddam Hussein to launch an armed attack on the United States and Australia in February 2003 as it was by then clear that Iraq was about to be attacked.

A second legal justification for the invasion of Iraq invoked by the United States related also to the threat of weapons of mass destruction, but had a more technical basis. This was the argument that a series of Security Council resolutions adopted over the last twelve years could be read to allow individual nations to invade Iraq to destroy its stocks of chemical, biological and possibly nuclear weapons.

The argument relied on by the coalition of the willing was that the war had the implicit approval of the UN Security Council. The approval was found in a combination of resolutions: 678 (passed in 1990) which sanctioned the use of force after Iraq's invasion of Kuwait; 687 (1991) which set out the ceasefire terms; and 1441 (2002) which dealt with strengthening the procedures to monitor Iraq's disposal of its weapons of mass destruction.

Australia's formal legal justification for joining the coalition of the willing rested on this 'continuing Security Council authorisation' rationale.

At the legal level, the attempt to locate a 'continuing authorisation' for war involved a selective and quite misleading interpretation of the Security Council resolutions. Words were taken from Security Council resolutions free of context to be given quite new meanings. In effect, the coalition of the willing argued that, because force had been authorised to remove Iraq from Kuwait in 1990, force could again be used to ensure that Saddam's regime had destroyed all weapons of mass destruction.

This interpretation went against the clear wording of the resolutions. It ignored the fact that the UN Special Commission (UNSCOM) and its successor, the UN Monitoring, Verification and Inspection Commission (UNMOVIC), had been established by the Security Council to monitor Iraq's compliance with the requirement that it destroy its stocks of particular weapons and that UNMOVIC was confident that progress had been made. The coalition's interpretation of Resolution 1441 in particular ignored the fact that an early version of that resolution prepared by the United States authorised the use of force if Iraq did not adequately comply with its terms, but that version was withdrawn because it did not command the Security Council's support. Statements made by both the United States and the United Kingdom at the time of the adoption of Resolution 1441 also specifically denied that it could be read as a 'trigger' for military intervention.

Part of the justification for the implausible interpretation of the Security Council resolutions was of course the United States' and United Kingdom's great public confidence that Iraq held significant stocks of biological and chemical weapons. The idea seemed to be, 'How can we let nice legal interpretations of words stand in the way of dealing with a crazed government sitting on a stockpile of dangerous weapons?' We now know that the claims about Iraq's possessions of weapons of mass destruction were at least exaggerated and based on surprisingly skimpy evidence. US Under-Secretary for Defense, Paul Wolfowitz, has indeed confided to *Vanity Fair* that the weapons of mass destruction issue was simply chosen as lead rationale for the invasion of Iraq for 'bureaucratic reasons'. It appears that the leaders of the coalition of the willing did not check the evidence very closely and that, even if signs of these weapons are now found, the great spectre of fear in March 2003 was largely manufactured. Enthusiasm for the invasion for a host of other reasons seems to have overrun a cautious appraisal of the facts.

A third legal rationale for the invasion was the argument that the international legal community had a duty to intervene in order to save the people of Iraq from the terrible dictator Saddam Hussein. For example, you may recall our own prime minister's speech in March 2003 committing Australia to the coalition of the willing when he spoke of the atrocities of Saddam's regime, particularly the gouging out of the eyes of children. More recently, Mr Howard has told troops returning from Iraq that they had fought in a just cause to save the people of Iraq from a dictator.

This type of argument is known by international lawyers as the doctrine of humanitarian intervention. Given the well-documented serious human rights violations of Saddam Hussein's rule, is there not a right, even a duty, for other nations to intervene to remove the source of the violations? The doctrine of humanitarian intervention was invoked in the case of the NATO bombings of Serbia in 1999. The idea then was that using military force against Serbia was the only way to ensure the protection of the Kosovar Albanians.

Many commentators have pointed out that the coalition of the willing's concern for the welfare of the Iraqi people was a very recent development and that the west sat by in the 1980s when Saddam engaged in massacres of his own people. We know that many western countries supplied Saddam with weapons and were indifferent to his capricious atrocities. Politically at least it seemed inconsistent suddenly to be developing a deep concern about the human rights of Iraqis. But these political inconsistencies may not have legal implications. After all, international lawyers have generally accepted Australia's intervention in East Timor in 1999 during the terrible post-election violence, despite our long history of supporting Indonesia's invasion and occupation of that island.

Does international law, then, allow one country to intervene in another if there are serious human rights abuses? The doctrine is at first sight a challenge to the basic principles of state sovereignty and non-intervention in the affairs of other countries so cherished under international law. What *are* the conditions required for humanitarian intervention?

An independent commission established by the Canadian government (co-chaired by former Australian Foreign Minister, Gareth Evans), the International Commission on Intervention and State Sovereignty, has recommended that the concept of 'humanitarian intervention' should be better characterised as a 'responsibility to protect'. The Commission noted that this change in terminology 'implies an evaluation of the issues from the point of view of those seeking or needing support, rather than those who may be considering intervention.'

The Commission's report attempted to find a balance between respect for state sovereignty and the need to respond to significant human rights violations. It articulated a responsibility to protect that may involve military intervention in international law and distilled three guiding principles. First, there must be a just cause. The Commission said: 'Military intervention for human protection purposes is an exceptional and extraordinary measure. To be warranted, there must be serious and irreparable harm occurring to human beings, or imminently likely to occur.' The Commission identified two types of such harm as a large-scale loss of life or a large-scale ethnic cleansing.

Second, the Commission stated that the primary purpose of the intervention must be to avert human suffering; that intervention can be justified only when every other non-military option has been explored; that the scale, duration and intensity of the military intervention should be the minimum necessary to protect; and that there must be a reasonable chance of averting the suffering that has justified the intervention.

The third principle identified by the Commission was that of 'right authority'. It argued that the UN Security Council was the most appropriate body in the first instance to authorise military intervention. If the Security Council were to reject a proposal for intervention, or fail to deal with it in a reasonable time, the Commission proposed that the UN General Assembly consider the matter under the 1950 Uniting for Peace Resolution which allows it to vote to support measures for the maintenance of international peace; or that action be taken by a regional organisation such as the African Union or ASEAN.

Measured against the criteria proposed by the International Commission on Intervention and State Sovereignty, the humanitarian intervention argument in the case of Iraq appears shaky. First, there was no public evidence of an actual or imminent large-scale loss of life caused by the Iraqi government. Sadly, there was much evidence of atrocities that occurred some time ago, while the west averted its gaze. Australia's own treatment of Iraqi asylum-seekers, challenging the validity of their claims of persecution, also undermines our claims that we invaded Iraq on human rights grounds.

Second, there was little evidence to suggest that the intention behind the coalition's intervention was to halt or avert human suffering. The consistently expressed intention (as it now appears, one whose basis was more the result of spin doctoring than fact) was the fear that Iraq's weapons of mass destruction would fall into the hands of terrorists. Indeed, there had been little international pressure brought on Saddam to treat his citizens better at any stage and so it is hard to argue that measures short of a military invasion to protect Iraqi human rights would not have succeeded. If the human rights of the Iraqis were the primary motive for the invasion, given the destruction of civilian life and infrastructure that it caused, questions can be raised about whether the means used to protect Iraqi human rights were proportionate.

Third, the 'right authority' requirement of the responsibility to protect proposed by the International Commission was not met. Of course, members of the coalition of the willing did try to get Security Council support for the intervention, but found little enthusiasm among the fifteen Security Council members. The lack of support went beyond what the United States regarded as the irresponsible use of the threat of the veto by France.

An important aspect of the 'responsibility to protect' formulation of the International Commission on Intervention and State Sovereignty is that it involves a responsibility to prevent conflict by dealing with root causes, a responsibility to react to situations of compelling human need and a responsibility to rebuild after any military intervention. In other words, humanitarian intervention cannot be seen as a right to be invoked when a country finds it convenient to do so. Taking the responsibility to protect formula seriously raises troubling questions for the international community and of course for us in Australia. For example, what does it signify in the case of the human rights situation in countries with which we have significant relationships, such as

Zimbabwe or Burma? What about the massacres and possibly genocide occurring in the Congo and Liberia?

My argument is that, from an international law perspective, there were serious problems with all the asserted legal rationales for the war on Iraq. But does this matter? Clearly, it did little to constrain the actions of the coalition of the willing. In any event, members of the coalition all produced legal opinions saying that there were valid grounds to go to war without Security Council authorisation. If there are views supporting both sides of a legal argument, how can we say that one side is better than another? One test an international lawyer might apply is to analyse the type of legal argumentation being used and to ask how an authoritative body such as the International Court of Justice might resolve the issues. On this test the coalition's various legal advices would seem very unpersuasive. Australia's legal advice, for example, does not cite any cases that support its reading of the various Security Council resolutions.

In any event, we have been urged by our political leaders to abandon discussion of the legality of the war and to focus on the fact that the war has been won. Many commentators have also seen the end of direct fighting between armies as an occasion to demand that critics of the war apologise for their misguided views. It is hard to predict now whether the failure to produce evidence to support the central public justification for the war against Iraq will carry a political price here in Australia. We know that the equally problematic dissembling at the heart of the 'children over-board' affair has had little effect on the government's popularity.

Despite its passionate denunciations of the Iraq government's possession of weapons of mass destruction before the invasion, the Australian government has since moved away from that justification for war to emphasise the new-found freedom of the Iraqi people in a post-Saddam Iraq. Indeed Mr Howard has followed President Bush in presenting the invasion as 'the best opportunity in a long time to achieve a lasting settlement in the ongoing and painful dispute between the state of Israel and the Palestinians'.[1]

Means and methods of warfare

The principles relating to the decision to use military force are known by international lawyers as the *ius ad bellum*. By contrast, the *ius in bello* comprises the rules relating to the means and methods of warfare. Sometimes people are surprised to learn that there are international laws governing the conduct of hostilities, believing the old adage that all's

---

1   Quoted in Patrick Walters, 'Farewell to Arms', *Weekend Australian* 7–8 June 2003, p 24.

fair in love and war. The major laws in this area are the four Geneva Conventions on the laws of war of 1949 and their two additional Protocols of 1977. They set out basic standards for the conduct of warfare, dealing with issues such as treatment of prisoners of war and treatment of civilians.

These issues emerged during the conduct of hostilities in Iraq—for example, the Iraqis were said to have used the red cross emblem in perfidious ways to trick their enemy into believing that military missions were humanitarian. There were also legal questions over the depiction of prisoners of war. Both sides in the conflict used images of prisoners of war in their propaganda battles in possible violation of Article 13 of the Third Geneva Convention that prohibits holding prisoners of war up to 'insults and public curiosity'.

The major method of ensuring compliance with the laws of armed conflict lies in its reciprocal nature. In other words, it's worth treating enemy prisoners with respect in the hope that prisoners from your own side will receive the same treatment. In this context, a major legal issue emerged for the United States during the course of the war in Iraq because of its treatment of Taliban and al Qaeda prisoners held at Guantanamo Bay in Cuba. If these prisoners were denied the procedures of the Third Geneva Convention, it became more difficult for the United States to insist on strict compliance with the treaty for its troops.

Other important principles of international humanitarian

law include the prohibitions on targeting civilian populations and civilian infrastructure and on causing extensive destruction of property not justified by military objectives. Intentionally launching an attack knowing that it will cause 'incidental' loss of life or injury to civilians 'which would be clearly excessive in relation to the concrete and direct overall military advantage anticipated' constitutes a war crime at international law. We do not yet have all the evidence about the actual conduct of the hostilities in Iraq, but the principles of international humanitarian law should make us scrutinise the conduct of all sides.

The fact that it now appears that the threat posed by Iraq was much less than our leaders insisted before the war, and that it seems our leaders should have known that the intelligence they relied on was deeply flawed, is particularly significant in such scrutiny. Given that the stated military objective of the coalition of the willing was to disarm Iraq and, given the lack of objective evidence of Iraq's stocks of weapons of mass destruction before the invasion, questions can now be raised about the legality of the widespread harm caused to the Iraqi population in the invasion. There is some suggestion that the United States used cluster bombs in the assault on Iraq, which would be a clear violation of humanitarian law.

The Geneva Conventions rely on national prosecutions for their enforcement. In other words, countries are expected to prosecute their own citizens for grave violations of the Geneva Conventions. This is usually highly unlikely because there will be very little political impetus for a government to charge its own soldiers for actions during armed conflict. The creation of the International Criminal Court in 2002 has, however, provided a stronger system of scrutiny and adjudication of violations of humanitarian law. The International Criminal Court now has jurisdiction over genocide, war crimes and crimes against humanity when national legal systems have not dealt with these crimes adequately. It attributes criminal responsibility to individuals responsible for planning military action that violates international humanitarian law and those who carry it out. It specifically extends criminal liability to heads of state, leaders of governments, parliamentarians, government officials and military personnel. The court came into operation in July 2003. Although the United States and Iraq have both refused to accept the jurisdiction of the court, the other members of the coalition of the willing, including Australia, are parties to the International Criminal Court's Statute. The court has already been asked to adjudicate on whether war crimes or crimes against humanity were committed during the war on Iraq. Although the outcomes of these cases will not be clear for some time, the existence of the International Criminal Court offers a new form of enforcement of the guarantees of humanitarian law.

The reconstruction of Iraq

International law is relevant also to current operations in Iraq. International law sets out the various responsibilities of an occupying power in the Fourth Geneva Convention of 1949. One fundamental duty is to restore and ensure public order and safety (Article 6). We know that, despite the official language of liberation, daily life is much less secure than it was under the Saddam regime. The coalition of the willing failed to plan adequately for the inevitable breakdown of law and order after their successful military operation. A report by Human Rights Watch in June 2003 claims that the coalition has not communicated with the local population about security; it has not deployed international police or judicial personnel; it has relied on combat troops for policing duties without adequate training; and it hasn't protected victims and witnesses in criminal matters. Ironically many Iraqis are now calling for the old corrupt and brutal police force to provide security. The medical situation in Iraq is much worse than before the war: there is no functioning health ministry and water shortages have caused cholera as families drink from rivers that contain sewage. The United Nations Children's Fund has estimated that 7.7 per cent of Iraqi children under five are now suffering from acute malnutrition, almost double the rate before the war began.

Officially, Iraq is now in a phase of reconstruction. The

coalition of the willing retains many troops in Iraq and it has established an authority to oversee the reconstruction led by former US diplomat L. Paul Bremer III. In May 2003 the United Nations Secretary-General appointed the former UN Administrator in East Timor, Sergio Viera de Mello, as his Special Adviser on Iraq. He was killed in August 2003 after an attack on United Nations headquarters in Baghdad.

At first sight, the plans for reconstruction seem to go beyond what is acceptable at international law. The Fourth Geneva Convention provides that an occupying power must preserve as far as possible the existing governmental and legal system of the occupied country. The idea is that occupation of another country must be temporary. However, the United Nations Security Council adopted a lengthy resolution (1483) on the reconstruction of Iraq on 22 May 2003 which goes beyond the 'no change' rule of the Fourth Geneva Convention. This resolution was hailed as a great compromise by the members of the Security Council who were critical of the war because it acknowledges the fact of US control over Iraq.

Although the text of Resolution 1483 refers to the Fourth Geneva Convention, it in fact goes far beyond the terms of the treaty. It endorses a sweeping role for what it terms 'the Authority', the coalition, with a subsidiary role to be played by the UN and an interim Iraqi administration (to be created primarily by the coalition). The coalition is called on to create 'conditions in which the Iraqi people can freely determine their own political future' and, with the UN, to 'establish national and local institutions for representative governance'. This departure from the traditional 'hands off' international legal principles relevant to occupying powers seems justified in the current situation where there is no clear alternative government. To allow a corrupt political and legal system to remain in place in Iraq would undermine the one undoubted benefit of the invasion, the removal of a cruel dictator from power.

There are, however, some aspects of Resolution 1483 that give pause. It sets no timetable for the handover of power to the Iraqi people. Iraq's main political groups have been critical of Paul Bremer for his slowness to create an interim administration. In July 2003, an Iraqi Governing Council was finally appointed by Mr Bremer. There remains concern that an extended occupation by the United States might turn the Iraqi population against the coalition and strengthen the Baath Party of Saddam Hussein.

Another concern with Resolution 1483 is that the Authority, rather than the UN, is given power to disburse the proceeds of the sale of Iraqi oil. Although the resolution requires that the funds be used to benefit the people of Iraq, the benefit is to be judged by the coalition of the willing, leading to the disturbing likelihood that the coalition will use the funds to pay its own corporations to repair the infrastructure that coalition forces themselves destroyed. It is also striking that Resolution 1483 calls for income to the Development Fund for Iraq to be independently audited, but not expenditures. The resolution cancels all existing legal rights to Iraq's oil, giving the coalition the right to sell the oil to whomever they choose.

The resolution also contains language that suggests that the future contemplated for Iraq will be cast in a very specific model of democracy, based on a free-market economy. Indeed Donald Rumsfeld told the Council on Foreign Relations in May 2003 that a liberated Iraq must move to privatise its state-owned enterprises. Resolution 1483 also contains some significant silences. It endorses the notion of a 'representative' government, but gives no clue as to who should be represented. US officials often refer to the need for representation of the Kurds, the majority Shiite Muslims and the Sunni Muslims. But what, for example, of representation on the basis of sex? A conference of Iraqi exiles convened by the United States in May 2003 included four women among the three hundred delegates. Of the twenty-five members of the interim Governing Council, three are women. In 2000, to much fanfare, the Security Council adopted Resolution 1325 which acknowledged the importance of women's equal participation in peace negotiations at all levels, but this resolution has not been put into practice in Iraq.

Another silence in Resolution 1483 is the measures to be taken to protect human rights or to provide justice and accountability for past violations of human rights. For example, how will responsibility for the mass graves being uncovered be determined? It is clear that the Iraqi judiciary does not have the capacity to deal with cases of this complexity.

Members of the coalition of the willing regularly cite Afghanistan as a model for the type of democratic reconstruction they plan in Iraq. For example, Australia's Foreign Minister, Mr Downer, spoke of the value of the Bonn conference in December 2001 in establishing the framework for a post-Taliban Afghanistan. Afghanistan is, however, a very worrying precedent for Iraq and my fear is precisely that the two will have similar experiences. Afghanistan is an example of squandered US enthusiasm for rebuilding a country. The security situation in Afghanistan is now reportedly even worse than under the Taliban government. Afghani prime minister Hamid Karzai is referred to as the 'Mayor of Kabul' indicating how narrow his area of influence and control is. It seems as though the US has lost enthusiasm about making Operation Enduring Freedom live up to its name, and disarmament programs in Afghanistan are being scaled back. Warlords have reasserted their authority with impunity. This precedent suggests some doubts about whether the US will stay the course on Iraq.

Various officials in the US administration and experts in Washington think-tanks regard Iraq as a potential bulwark of democracy in the Middle East. They have developed what has been termed a 'tsunami' theory of Iraqi democracy. The idea is that a reconstructed Iraq could become a model for the region, which will then be unable to resist the great wave of democracy. This optimism seems quite misplaced at the moment, but it also ignores the fact that any Iraqi democracy engineered by the coalition will not be seen as a local model: many Arabs will regard Iraq as 'liberated' through western intervention, rather than by a powerful local movement.

Conclusion

From the perspective of international law, the decision to go to war in Iraq, the conduct of the war and its aftermath are problematic. The Italian jurist Antonio Cassese has described two opposing tendencies in the international legal order that are relevant to Iraq. Cassese terms the first tendency the Westphalian, a reference to the Treaty of Westphalia in 1648, which is taken as the starting point of the modern international community of states. The major features of the Westphalian order are that:

- there is great emphasis on national sovereignty and a reluctance to acknowledge external powers;

- force is the primary source of legitimation;
- legal functions (such as dispute resolution and law enforcement) are decentralised;
- the right to resort to force is unfettered.

Cassese has said of the Westphalian model that 'The resulting picture is that of a community where law does not place any restraint on power…[and] [e]conomic, social and military inequalities fail to be taken into account.' The second tendency identified by Cassese is the Charter order, a reference to the principles of the UN Charter adopted in 1945. The Charter order is characterised by:

- the growth of international institutions;
- concern with human rights of individuals;
- sweeping restrictions on the use of force;
- development of universal norms of conduct and a concern with justice rather than power.

Cassese makes the important observation that the Charter order has not completely displaced the Westphalian order and that the two co-exist in uneasy tension in international society. The war in Iraq and its aftermath represent the triumph of a Westphalian order. They undermine the idea that there is an international rule of law, where like cases are treated alike and where a system of justice restrains arbitrary action. We can see now in Iraq, as in Afghanistan before it, that military successes do not always have the desired results.

The fall of Saddam Hussein's Iraq was presented by its supporters as a way to reduce the threat of terrorism. But it is clear that the invasion has encouraged a new generation of people without any form of power to resent the military might of the west.

So, has Iraq been a success or failure in international legal terms? Should we see it as a disaster for international law, a rent in the delicate fabric that has taken centuries to develop and which may keep tearing? Some international lawyers have read Iraq as the death of the system of collective security set out in the UN Charter. Others point to the continuing significance of the UN; at least the US felt constrained to go to the UN, the argument runs, even if it ultimately ignored it.

I think that the war on Iraq, with its aftermath, has shaken the foundations of international law, but at the same time it has underlined the real value of the international legal system. I don't want to exaggerate the virtues of international law or claim that it is the answer to all geopolitical problems. It has many blindspots. It is particularly inadequate in dealing with structural injustices. But perhaps the greatest asset of international law is its insistence (albeit hard to realise in many contexts) on a collective, rather than an individualised, notion of justice. It offers a set of standards against which we can measure international behaviour and call governments to account.

The price of ignoring international law in the case of Iraq is that it will be much harder to invoke international legal standards when we want to restrain others. For example, the invasion of Iraq might be seen as a useful precedent for India to invade Pakistan on the basis of Pakistan's significant stocks of weapons of mass destruction—or vice versa.

But, at the end of the day, perhaps we do not need to use international law to measure the wrongness of the attack on Iraq and to analyse the chaos it created and the suffering it caused. The ill-thought-out decisions that launched this attack are strikingly captured, not by legal principles, but in the arts—especially by visual images and in poetry.

I'd like to end by quoting part of a poem by the Chilean writer Ariel Dorfman. When Colin Powell presented his PowerPoint case against Iraq in the Security Council on 5 February 2003, a tapestry version of Picasso's great painting depicting the horror of war, *Guernica*, which hangs in the Security Council chamber, was covered up, apparently to provide a less distracting visual background when Mr Powell faced the media.

Dorfman's poem is called 'Pablo Picasso Has Words for Colin Powell from the Other Side of Death':

> *...It had been covered, our Guernica,*
> *covered so you could speak.*
> *There in the United Nations building.*
> *So you could speak about Iraq.*

Undisturbed by Guernica.
Why should it disturb perturb you?
Why did you not ask that the cover
 be removed
   the picture
 be revealed?
Why did you not point to the shrieking
the horse dying over and over again
the woman with the child forever dead
the child that I nurse here in this darkness
the child who watches with me
as you speak
 and you speak.
Why did you not say
This is why we must be rid of the dictator.
Why did you not say
This is what Iraq has already done and undone.
Why did you not say
This is what we are trying to save the world from.
…
Were you afraid that the horse
would show the world the near future
three thousand cruise missiles in the first hour
spinning into Baghdad
ten thousand Guernicas
spinning into Baghdad
  from the sky

Were you afraid of my art
        what I am still saying
more than sixty five years later
the story still being told
the vision still dangerous
the light bulb still hanging
        like an eye from the dead...[2]

Bibliography

Advice on the Use of Force against Iraq (containing both the Commonwealth government's legal advice and that of the Australian Labor Party) 4 *Melbourne Journal of International Law* 178 (2003).

Antonio Cassese, *International Law in a Divided World* (1986).

The Responsibility to Protect: Report of the International Commission on Intervention and State Sovereignty (December 2001).

Human Rights Watch, *Basra: Crime and Insecurity under British Occupation* (3 June 2003).

---

2   'Pablo Picasso Has Words for Colin Powell from the Other Side of Death' is available on-line at http://www.opendemocracy.net/themes/article-1-1002.jsp

AFTERMATH

Eva Sallis

As Iraqi Americans reach out to their relatives in Baghdad and Basra, in Kirkuk and Irbil, some are hearing words they never thought possible: Iraqis are speaking ill of Saddam Hussein. They're criticising him out loud, on the telephone, seemingly undeterred by fear of the Iraqi intelligence service and its tactics of torture for those disloyal to the Baath Party regime. 'I was shocked,' said Zainab Al Suwaij, executive director of the American Islamic Congress. 'It's very dangerous. All the phones are tapped. But they are so excited.'

Los Angeles Times, 24 March 2003

Ajami Saadoun Khlis, whose son and brother were executed under the Saddam regime, sobbed like a child on the shoulder of the *Guardian*'s Egyptian translator. He mopped the tears but they kept coming. 'You just arrived,' he said. 'You're late. What took you so long? God help you become victorious. I want to say hello to Bush, to shake his hand. We came out of the grave.'

Guardian, 22 March 2003

We shall never forget what the coalition has done for our people. A free Iraq shall be a living monument to our people's friendship with its liberators.

Hojat al Islam Abdel Majid al Khoi,
Wall Street Journal, 7 April 2003

People, if you only knew what this man did to Iraq. He killed our youth. He killed millions.

An elderly man in Baghdad beating Saddam's portrait with his shoe, *Los Angeles Times*,
10 April 2003[1]

These personal testimonies of Iraqis are among the most powerful and memorable of all defences for the war on Iraq. They are real, not hypothetical. They remind us of the human gains, not the cost. They make us feel that we were there with a purpose. We helped to remove Saddam Hussein. We can choke up at what it means to have helped free these people from such horror. We can feel good. I think for many Australians there is a kind of intimacy with these voices, a direct involvement, for we were part of their liberation.

Nonetheless, an unresolved question hangs over our goodness. We have a vested interest in engaging with these Iraqis' voices and not with those who are critical of us. The

---

1   These are collated, along with many others in the discussion following, from an article at http://www.freerepublic.com/focus/f-news/891424/ posts?page=24

discomfort I have with the emotional and intellectual argument Iraqis' relief presents to us is that we make each voice representative of all, including the dead. We habitually, uncritically, substitute the life of one Iraqi for another. We so easily hold these voices up as emblems, rather than hearing them as personal experiences, personal opinions. We so easily make these words speak for the dead and assuage our guilt, and we say: *See, it was all for this. Such relief was achieved by our killings!* In short, we sacrificed some Iraqis so that many might be saved. That is an age-old and very comforting argument.

But these individual voices, no matter how numerous, cannot speak for the dead. They cannot replace the voices of those people we never met or heard. The voices of relief cannot suggest that those who died did so as willing sacrifices. They cannot answer all questions on our right to kill. They cannot remove our responsibility for the killing, even if they reassure us that it was not without positive outcome for those who survived.

> When they started taking us off the bus…my mother told me 'repeat the Shahada, because we are about to die.' I heard the shouting of the children. We grabbed each other's hands—me, my mother, my cousin, and my uncle. They pulled us, we were all together. They threw us into the dugout grave…there were so many bodies underneath me. I layed down on top of them. They started to

shoot on us…One of them pulled at my clothes and said, 'this one isn't dead, shoot him.' They shot again, but still I was not shot. So they gave the order to the bulldozer driver to bury the grave. It was sundown now. I crawled to the edge of the grave and got to a place where the bamboo was on my face and I was able to breathe through it.

Nasir Khadi Hazim al Husseini, survivor, aged twelve in 1991[2]

Every day that uncovers more mass graves is a demonstration that there's a huge humanitarian and moral dividend out of what took place, and that it was right in terms of Australia's participation.

John Howard, Prime Minister of Australia[3]

The evidence of mass graves is another powerful defence of the war that is gaining momentum now as the likelihood of finding weapons of mass destruction fades. We are offered the grief shown at the opening of a mass grave as proof of the crimes of the regime we have removed. Iraqis' voices cry out over innumerable piles of bones. They reveal to us some of the horrors of Saddam Hussein's regime. We take these killings as reassurance—the graves help establish a proxy

---

2   'The Mass Graves of al Muhawil: The Truth Uncovered: VIII A Survivor' Human Rights Watch Report 2003.
3   Catherine McGrath, 'Forged document used as justification for Iraq war causing a stir' Monday, 7 July 2003, ABC Online.

mandate in the absence of a clear justification at law. The war was an ending of bloodshed, we are told, a peacekeeping style of intervention that has precedents when the killing in a country has become too shocking for the international community to stand idly by and let it happen.

Can these horrors really make us feel that we killed for a greater good? Undoubtedly they can. The effect they have on politicians and on TV viewers and newspaper readers is evidence enough of this. But I don't think they should make us feel that the subject is closed or that we should rest easy. The grief at mass graves is not for those we killed. There is no causal relationship between the person killed by Saddam Hussein and the person killed by us.

We would feel less ease if our media were keen to take us again and again to the funerals of those we did kill. I have been watching Arabic television via satellite throughout the last few months, and there is little comfort or self-congratulation possible at those other gravesides.

I think the killings in the recent war need to be thought through more deeply and considered beyond what makes us comfortable. All this scrabbling for comfort and self-congratulation has at its source a profound and unscrutinised discomfort with what we have done and are doing.

★

In 1991, Robert Gates, deputy national security adviser to that other Bush administration, stated that as long as Saddam Hussein remained in power, the sanctions would be enforced and, he said, 'Iraqis will pay the price.'

In 1996, Madeleine Albright, then US Ambassador to the United Nations, was asked whether half a million dead Iraqi children were a price worth paying for the gains of the embargo. In a statement now famous in the Middle East, she replied, 'I think this is a very hard choice, but the price—we think the price is worth it.'[4] There were still seven years of the embargo to go.

In 2003, as part of the war on terror (President Bush's 'monumental struggle between good and evil'[5]), a US-led coalition of just a handful of countries invaded Iraq, ousted Saddam Hussein and will remain there for the foreseeable future as occupying forces. At least 7376[6] civilians have been killed, alongside uncounted tens of thousands of men and boys who either defended the regime, or defended the country.

In the heated debates before the war on Iraq, collective self-defence from the global threat of Saddam Hussein, collective liberation or rescue of the oppressed Iraqi people

---

4   Both quoted in Andrew and Patrick Cockburn, *Saddam Hussein: An American Obsession*, Verso, 2002 p. 138; p. 264.
5   Quoted in Bob Woodward, *Bush at War*, Simon & Schuster, 2002 p. 45.
6   Iraq Body Count minimum figure as at 6 October 2003, http:// www.iraqbodycount.net/

and the irredeemable badness of the bad men at the top, particularly Saddam Hussein, were key features in persuading governments and individuals to support America's war. At a popular level, in the United States, 'payback' or vengeance for September 11 also played a part.[7] Most, if not all, supporters of the war saw this as going to get Saddam Hussein for the west's sake and/or for the sake of the Iraqi people. It turned out that the latter was a stronger argument, but it is interesting that in the lead-up to the war almost every justification for killing a human being that has any currency in western cultures was used to argue that we should kill or bring Saddam Hussein to justice, necessarily killing any number of Iraqis to do so. On an emotional level, we went to war against one man.

Worldwide demonstrations against the war offered a spectacular picture of the discomfort millions (including me) felt over this. But the demonstrations did nothing to counter the threat those who supported the war felt, and filled with dismay those Iraqis who saw the war as a possible solution to their nightmare. That Saddam Hussein was so bad, so corrupt, as to deserve our uncompromising aggression was a shared view but invading his country and inevitably killing Iraqis to get to him was a subject of intense disagreement.

It is in the past now. We have been a participant in the

---

7   According to a February 2003 poll, 72% of Americans think Iraq was linked to the September 11 attacks, despite no evidence of its involvement.

killing that ousted Saddam Hussein and his regime and liberated the Iraqi people from him, if not, so far, from us. Whatever it is that has taken place (we are unsure, still) we are responsible for it.

There still seems to be much that is unsaid on this war. Supporters talk about successes: minimum civilian casualties, the overthrow of Saddam, the opportunity we have given Iraqis and the proof that weapons of mass destruction existed sometime in the past, and that it is only a matter of time before they are found. Objectors talk about the new American century and the numbers of civilians really killed, the numbers of ongoing killings, the uncounted military dead, and the mess we have made of Iraq, a country that is not going to be given back to the Iraqis any time soon. A debate still rages in the highest circles, particularly in Britain and the US, on whether the war was lawful, or otherwise justified. A panel of eminent lawyers confirmed in May that in their considered view this war was unlawful.[8]

We argue that we have killed fewer people in liberating Iraq than Saddam Hussein did in subjugating it.

This should be scrutinised if only for the fact we find it comforting.

It is easy to demonstrate, with the bewildering numbness

---

8   Severin Carrell and Robert Verkaik, 'War on Iraq was Illegal, Say Top Lawyers', *Independent* (UK), 25 May 2003.

of statistics, that America and its allies are responsible directly and indirectly for the deaths of far more Iraqis than Saddam Hussein. No one could seriously believe the Bush administration's argument of compassion and concern for the well-being of the remaining living Iraqis. But whether in argument or counter-argument, the numbers we cite can escalate until they repel any proper engagement with what any of it means.

When we talk about minimum civilian casualties or an acceptable price to pay, we are using a language that neutralises the impact of our responsibility and cushions our grief. The numbers argument (how few we killed) has been used to soften uncomfortable fact to the point where it becomes comfortable. To me it seems to gloss with a positive light something we would find very painful to contemplate closely. It also functions as a last, defining word, a word that erases the diversity of human beings to which it refers. And it is extraordinarily flexible in function. There is no number of deaths that cannot be described as a 'minimum', no number of deaths that, if we are sufficiently insulated from their meaning, cannot be described as 'a price worth paying'. There is no maximum, no cut-off point, if we are sufficiently desensitised, as Madeleine Albright was, to the seriousness of killing one person.

Any number of deaths was acceptable to Saddam Hussein as a means to information, control, and, in the 1970s, development and progress for Iraq. If we are going to defend our actions with our minimum killed, we do need to have some kind of cut-off point that distinguishes us from a man we consider so morally reprehensible that we invaded his country and killed people in order to remove him from power. The impact of sanctions on the citizens of Iraq was catastrophic and had no cut-off point. In this war, as I will show, we have no cut-off point, just a vague notion that we did all we could to keep civilian deaths to a minimum.

Curiously, if I were to suggest a low cut-off point, say five acceptable killings, they have much greater impact. We identify with the humanity of five people easily. What is apparent and immediate in the killing of five people is their uniqueness, their individuality. Even if they are strangers or enemies, we recognise this. We are more easily repelled by the idea of killing five people as an acceptable sacrifice than we are by 7376. This demonstrates the danger of this numbers argument. It disengages the faculty of identification, precisely the faculty that needs to be activated if we are to contemplate the full meaning of our actions.

It is commonplace to show that Americans care about Americans. As we would expect, their recognition of the seriousness of the loss of life of their compatriots is fully developed. Had any Australian soldiers died, we would have seen exactly the same recognition by Australians. Cameraman Paul Moran's death in Iraq is mourned with a full awareness of the great loss of his unique life. The number of American soldiers killed, tallied almost daily in the ongoing guerrilla war in Iraq, was becoming unacceptable to the American public at the 23 August 2003 figure of 179. (The administration, conscious of the impact of these numbers, separates those killed in combat from those who died in non-combat situations. The total number of US military deaths at the same date was 273.)

It is clearly possible to count the dead with pain and recognition and grief. We might have misused numbers, but they are still important. For many Australians, numbers are our only link with these deaths, our only point of contact.

What would it mean if we didn't bother to count?

We didn't count the Iraqi military dead, a fact that stuns me every time I come up against it. We could have killed 10,000 or 100,000 men and boys (and a few women) and it would mean nothing to us. 'Military targets' were not presented to us through the media as dead in the same way as killed civilians were. Our moral well-being was felt to be related to the number of civilian dead, but completely untouched by either the number or nature of military dead. A loose tally was kept by a few organisations for the one, but not for the other.

Why are the military dead treated as though there is no question that this war was just and lawful? Why are there so few voices of outrage at this? Men and boys who were killed while they defended their country or defended the regime we were destroying have been made invisible as though their deaths do not reflect upon us or invoke our understanding of right and wrong. This is an extraordinary sleight of hand. Their deaths do in the clearest terms invoke a questioning of right and wrong, even a resolution, once and for all, concerning the lawfulness of this war. We all know that a soldier's job in war is to kill. This sense of the inevitability of death in warfare can help to obscure how seriously we should question our right to kill in this war, and how seriously we should scrutinise our view of the killing of these men and boys.

There is a difference between civilian and military deaths. It is not a difference that can, in the context of this war, erase the question of right and wrong, but one that has considerable impact on our thoughts and feelings. Civilian deaths were accidental, unintended. Military deaths were intentional. To remove Saddam Hussein, we had to fight and wound or kill those who actively opposed us. But just because they actively defended a country we invaded should not lead to such a complete failure to recognise the killing of the defenders. This should not render them invisible, and leave them out of the questions we ask of ourselves.

Saddam Hussein killed several hundred thousand human beings in suppressing a major revolt against him in 1991 and, as far as we know, his administration kept meticulous records of names. We did not even do that and we have no idea how many we killed.

We wiped them off the face of the earth.

These killings were intended. We have a huge vested interest in ignoring them. It was an unjust war and these killings are, in moral terms, murders. If this war was indeed unlawful, then we have been part of the 'supreme international crime, differing only from other war crimes in that it contains within itself the accumulated evil of the whole.'[9]

It is a worse crime to kill two people than it is to kill one. But the meaning of killing human beings inheres in the significance of killing one person. The seriousness of ending a unique individual life is what makes killing three people worse than killing one. We cannot easily look for the meaning of mass killing, whether it is 7376, hundreds of thousands, or millions, without returning to the meaning of taking one life. All recent debate over acceptable numbers of killings as means to ends seems to me to depend upon a wilful refusal to consider the significance of killing.

The talk of minimum civilian casualties and an acceptable price as used to justify this war seems only tenable if we pretend killing one person is really not so terrible. Our failure to be outraged at the lost uncounted dead bears this out. It would be much harder to support such killing if someone you

---

9   *Nuremberg Trial Proceedings*, Volume 22, 217th day Monday, 30 September 1946, 'The Common Plan or Conspiracy and Aggressive War', http://www.yale.edu/lawweb/avalon/imt/proc/09-30-46.htm

love is automatically to be among the number you consider acceptable, or is to be lost and unacknowledged forever. We might have talked in a murky and imprecise way about rescuing people and about the suffering of Iraqis but we really positioned ourselves emotionally as enemies. These deaths we deemed acceptable, these deaths we choose not to know about, would never mean to us what the deaths of our own would.

Iraqis are far away for most Australians, but this distance increased, I think, our duty and the duty of our leaders to consider the meaning of what we were doing.

The culture of using one person as a means to an end reached, under Saddam Hussein, a kind of ultimate expression. I do not need to repeat the catalogue of unbearable acts that were both possible and permissible in the late stages of Saddam's Iraq. These are well known. But I would like to give a sense of the prevailing culture and what it meant to the bodies and lives of individuals. He stated in a memo to his heads of security in 1992:

> *Article 12E:* We call upon the interrogator to exercise patience while interrogating arrested elements, to enable us to identify and define our enemies. Those who died as a result of interrogation

methods are a loss…because we lost a link in our investigations which could have led us to their superior and his superiors. In fact, they were more patient than the interrogators even though they were facing death.

…

From Article 27: Even if we make a mistake in bringing in a citizen and subject him to torture without reaching any conclusion with him in obtaining information, I say to you that we have benefited from him in that he will describe the way he was arrested and the methods to which he was subjected even though innocent, then how would it have been if he had a conspiratorial or treasonous mind. Such conspiracy shall be a horror screen before his eyes, giving him sleepless nights, making him distance himself from even thinking about politics or hostility to the Revolution. He will also flee from anyone around him who may have inclinations of this nature.

…

Top Secret Memo: All Department Heads, Sector Officers, and Headquarters Branches Plan of Action 1992[10]

---

10 Full Memo available at Frontline's website, http://www.pbs.org/wgbh/pages/frontline/shows/saddam/readings/action.html

Saddam Hussein's regime was horrible and, in any comparison, we look better. Our actions and the extent of our power over the bodies and lives of individuals, citizens or non-citizens, are far from being equally or so extensively horrible. But comparison with something really nightmarishly terrible should not be our sole means of measuring our good.

In May 2003, Khraisan al Abally was released from detention in Baghdad.[11] US soldiers had stormed his home. According to the family, Khraisan's brother Dureid thought they were looters. He opened fire on them and was shot. Khraisan was arrested. The Americans apparently believed he knew the whereabouts of General Izzat al Douri, one of the high-ranking Baath Party officers. For eight days and nights Khraisan was forced to kneel semi-naked, hands and feet tied, with a blindfold or under strobe lights with incessant loud music playing. He was repeatedly interrogated and in the course of interrogation, he was told that his brother was dead. When released, his knees were bleeding and swollen. A month after his release, he still had welts where his wrists were tied.

Khraisan al Abally has lodged a complaint against his captors. Amnesty and Human Rights Watch have also begun an investigation. The US military response was an official

---

11 Jim Krane, 'Iraqi Details Harsh Treatment as Amnesty Criticises US Interrogation Method', Associated Press, 30 June 2003.

statement that its officers adhere to the rule of law. When questioned further, they stated that sleep deprivation, shackling prisoners in uncomfortable positions, noise abuse and from strobe lights are lawful interrogation aids. When questioned about Dureid al Abally, who is missing, they responded that they had no record of a person of that name.

The most disturbing part of this story is if we view it from Khraisan's point of view. His brother is dead or, at the very least, he believes his brother is dead. The killing of someone he loved is used as part of an interrogation that includes the kind of cruelty and humiliation that any reasonable person would recognise as torture. How is he supposed to tell the difference between how he was treated and how he might have been treated by Saddam Hussein's interrogators? In the world of this man's life, this man's individual experience, is there any real difference between the Americans and Saddam Hussein? If, in the light of this story, we are to maintain there is a difference, we would have to argue that it is a difference in the numbers of people subjected by us to such pain, but given that two Afghans have died under American interrogation from 'blunt force injuries', and given Khraisan al Abally's experience, it is hard to maintain an absolute difference in kind.[12] The Americans tortured

---

12 'The Threat of a Bad Example: Undermining International Standards as "War on Terror" Detentions Continue', Amnesty, *Ottawa Post*, 19 August 2003.

a man and killed a family member, or used the incidental killing of a family member, to get information from him. It was not an aberration: it was 'lawful'. It was, is, standard practice.

America has detained ten thousand Iraqis in prisons with no accountability and no outside scrutiny.[13] It has not even recorded all the prisoners' names. We know many more than Khraisan al Abally have been tortured, in lesser or greater degrees, in order to obtain information.

If we sanction at law the torturing of one person, allowing his or her torturers to act lawfully in inflicting humiliation and physical and emotional suffering, if we argue that we kill or torture fewer people than Saddam Hussein did, are we on unassailable territory for defending what we have done?

Where is the cut-off point going to be? At what point, at how many tortured, would torture become wrong if we allow it to be lawful at all?

A lot of what I have outlined above applies to so many wars that it could be seen to be an age-old and ineffectual

---

13 ABC News Online, September 17th 2003, 'US Admits Holding 10,000 Iraqi Prisoners' http://www.abc.net.au/news/newsitems/s947282.htm

discussion against killing, torture and warfare generally. To that I can only say that embarking without due thought on an unprovoked invasion and occupation of a country raises all these questions afresh, and that they need to be discussed in the context of our alliance with America and the judgments we made and make of Iraq. We Australians need to discuss what it means to move towards a world that sees one human life as an acceptable price to pay to get to another, and sees damaging one human body or mind as an acceptable means to obtain information or control, or to send a negative message to others. We need to discuss any shift we make from a notion of universal human rights, not just slide into something else without facing the nature of what we are doing.

Nothing I have said here can change the source of our acquiescence or active support for the war on Iraq. We are afraid. We are sufficiently afraid of 4000 Iraqi refugees to have supported and encouraged our government's decision to harm them a little to deter other Iraqis from asking for our help. We are sufficiently afraid of terrorism, of Islam, of the taint of Saddam Hussein, that we let ourselves see killing Iraqis as an acceptable price to pay for the perceived lessening of our fear and the increase of our safety. Without this fear, I can't see that we would have defended our actions in quite the same way—with all the trappings of enmity but no acknowledgment of it. We dehumanised Iraqis, spoke of them as collective victims or collective aggressors, while presenting ourselves as saviours or as agents of retribution. This seems to me to be enmity. Our fear made action an imperative, but we had to manufacture reasons for our fear, and reasons to act.

What if our fear was baseless? What if it came from us, from our lack of connection, understanding or identification with individual Iraqi experience? From our failure to feel our shared humanity? What if it was a phantom? What if we were duped, first of all by ourselves?

What have we let ourselves become?

It is too late to say that this is America, not us. We agreed that the United States should pursue its objectives in Iraq. We helped them do it. We joined our active will to theirs. We have not pressured our representatives to register any official dismay. We have not yet, at any point, said as a nation: *No! That is not what we meant at all.*

A LAST RESORT

Raimond Gaita

I

No ordinary, well-informed citizen of the nations that went to war against Iraq knows how many people were killed in that war. No one has bothered to tell us, if indeed anybody has found out, how many Iraqi soldiers were killed. It seems not to matter to our leaders or to our media. If it mattered to more of us, then perhaps it would matter to them.

When they compare the war in Iraq to many of the terrible wars of last century, some people—military historians or people fascinated by the grand strategies of geopolitics—might consider its human cost to be relatively small. Civilian casualities at any rate were not as high as was feared, partly because the coalition of the willing was looking over its shoulder at a world that was unfriendly to what it was doing and partly because Baghdad fell without the street fighting many had predicted. Supporters and opponents of the war both have reason to be glad that the sun shines on the just and on the unjust.

After World War II it seemed we had entered an era marked by ever-increasing acknowledgment that even in politics one could not so readily as in the past treat human beings as expendable, not even for a noble cause. Much of the struggle for human rights and for the development of international law—the unqualified prohibition against torture, for example—seemed to express that part of our tradition that taught that each human life is a miracle. During the build-up to the invasion all three leaders—George W. Bush, Tony Blair and John Howard—professed their belief that human life is sacred, and more than once implied that to support the war would be to protect that belief from evil-doers who had no understanding of it or who even despised it.

No one believed them of course—or at any rate, no one who could keep two thoughts in her mind for long enough to notice they were inconsistent. How can you expect anyone seriously to accept that you believe that every human life is sacred if, like the Howard government, you destroy, with unrelenting ruthlessness, the lives of many who seek asylum in this country, or if you bomb soldiers as mercilessly as the Americans do and then refuse to 'do body counts' (to quote Donald Rumsfeld). Our leaders invoked the sanctity of life partly because it tuned in with the moralistic/religious fundamentalism expressed often in other connections by George Bush, and with Tony Blair's astonishing admission that he would attack every brutal dictatorship in the world if only he could.

That tells us something of what they mean when they speak of the sanctity of human life. But, as leaders effectively engaged in secular rather than religious politics, they could speak of the sanctity of human life only because that idea has important secular expressions—that every human being is owed unconditional respect, is an end in herself and should never be treated merely as a means, for example. In both its religious and secular forms the idea (or perhaps better, the ideal) inspired the fight for human rights and for the development of international institutions to ensure that those who commit crimes against humanity are called to account. If I am right, then it is irony, bitter and heartbreaking, that our leaders should have appealed to belief in the sanctity of life in order to enlist support for a war whose prosecution showed so clearly how marginal that belief is in the politics of the nations that went to war.

The confidence of this Christian triumvirate that a moral justification for invading Iraq is to be found in the good achieved by it is evidently not disturbed by St Paul's injunction that evil must not be done though good may come of it, even though that injunction has been fundamental to Christian (and other) formulations of what counts as a just war. To be sure, that injunction has always been in (I think, irreconcilable) tension with politics. At certain points of crises politicians will always do morally terrible things if those

Is it more important than morality?

What is the root of these responsibilities.

things are necessary to safeguard the very conditions of political communality, and they will do so in sober acknowledgment of the responsibilities of a political vocation.

St Paul's injunction expresses an ethic of renunciation, but renunciation cannot be the way of politics, not at any rate at certain critical points of 'necessity' as they are often called. An ethic of renunciation need not have a religious basis. Socrates expressed it when he said that it is better to suffer evil than to do it. To his incredulous interlocutors, he acknowledged that nothing in morality, as he understood it, can save us from the possibility that we will face an enemy who is cunning enough to ensure that the only available means for our self-defence are evil. Morality, as Socrates understood it, may require us to renounce the means to achieve what we most passionately and decently desire, and the means to protect what we rightly cherish.

In some parts of our tradition the Socratic doctrine was deepened and transformed by an affirmation of the inalienable preciousness of every human being—even those whose deeds and hearts are so evil that we can find no place in them in which a sober remorse might grow. In its religious formulation, it affirms that every human life is sacred. Sometimes it is expressed in stories and parables that tell us that we are all God's children or that we are all created in God's image. Sometimes it is expressed in abstract theological and philosophical doctrines. It has secular formulations, the greatest of them by Immanuel Kant, who said that we must never treat others merely as a means to our ends, but always as ends in themselves. In its most sublime form, it affirms that even the most terrible evil-doers are owed unconditional respect.

Many people will, I know, be incredulous that I should speak of politics as a vocation at a time when it seems anachronistic to speak that way even of teaching or nursing. But politics can be a noble calling, and like nursing and teaching, its deepest responsibilities are discovered not in the idea of a career or a profession, but in the idea of a vocation or in a cognate idea. Readiness to do evil when it is necessary to safeguard the conditions of political communality is, as Max Weber put it, the most salient aspect of the 'ethic of responsibility' that defines a political vocation. But it defines it only when it is in genuine tension with what he called an 'ethic of absolute ends', which for my purposes (though not quite for his) can be expressed in St Paul's injunction or in the Socratic precept that it is better to suffer evil than to do it. Politics that avoids or subverts that tension declines into moralism of a kind that threatens the conditions of political communality or into reckless adventurism or into the ruthless pursuit of economic or strategic interests justified by appeal to necessity when none exists. Politicians must, as politicians, sometimes do what morally they must not do. That dilemma, soberly acknowledged, constitutes the misery and the dignity of a political vocation.

Unconditional respect for human life, reverence and awe in the face of its infinite preciousness, does not show itself in the mere fact that you try to kill as few civilians as possible when you wage war. It shows in the first instance in the reasons why you wage war. Only if you wage it as a last resort can you seriously claim that lives were unavoidably sacrificed and only the serious effort to avoid sacrificing even one life is consistent with claiming that each life is a miracle. That may sound like high-minded hyperbole: it should sound like a tautology.

Because no weapons of mass destruction have yet been found, the credibility of the claim that we had urgently to go to war as an act of preventive self-defence has become so implausible, even to supporters of the war, that our leaders now tell us that we were right to go in order to liberate the Iraqis. Never mind that Blair and Howard said before the war that the desirability of 'regime change' would not justify war against Saddam. But though our political leaders say we were right to go to war, I have not heard them say that we were (morally) obliged to go. Not one of them has suggested that the Iraqis could justifiably have claimed that we would have wronged them if we did not go. To support their justification of the invasion they point to the good achieved, avoiding as much as they can acknowledgment of the harm done. We have seen the mass graves and the tears of those who identified their relatives amongst the skeletons, but we have not seen the dismembered corpses in the trenches we bombed nor the tears of those who mourn them.

Avoidance of that acknowledgment is not, however, the point I want to stress against our leaders. To the contrary, it is that this merry band of Christians sees no need to appeal to anything beyond a balance of harms and benefits, as though there had never existed a long tradition, Christian and secular, that argued that weighing the consequences of what we do yields only a partial (moral) understanding of it. Sadly they are far from alone in this. Almost without exception the so-called humanitarian argument for the invasion has been put in terms which betray total amnesia of that tradition. That, I suppose, is why we also forget that the good we achieve by unjust means is polluted by those means.

Few people now believe the reasons we went to war are the reasons we were given. The real reason, many people believe understandably enough, was to serve the financial interests of the coalition—control of the oil fields and securing investment opportunities being merely the most obvious. But something that is more subversive even than realpolitik of our sense that every human life is precious motivated the coalition. All the leaders of the coalition seemed in thrall to the grand adventure of geopolitics, to the adventure of seizing a decisive moment in history in order radically to change the political structures of the Middle East, and perhaps even those of Africa and Asia. It is a perennial temptation. We admire it when we praise as great, heroic and noble the deeds of Caesar and Napoleon. From such a perspective the lives of ordinary people, especially of soldiers, are expendable. So much so that you don't even bother to count the dead.

No one knows what the consequences will be of the invasion of Iraq, not even for Iraq and its neighbours. The attitude to the US of many of the people who live in the Middle East and in other underdeveloped nations appears to be as complex as the US itself. They seem to hate, admire and envy America in a state of moral and psychic confusion potent enough to make anyone mad. Increasingly the Iraqis appear to be responding to their liberation (and liberation it truly was) with a similar unstable combination of attitudes. Geopolitical speculations will continue as they did before the war, and people will, as always, say they know things they do not know. None of the major political events of the last thirty years or so—certainly not in international affairs—was predicted. It is unlikely that in the next few years events in the Middle East will prove an exception.

Most opponents of the war will hope, without inconsistency, that America's desire for democracy to take root in Iraq and neighbouring states will be fulfilled. If, however, that hope is to be consistent with a sober desire to extend the influence and authority of international law, then, I think, opponents of the war must also hope that the US and Britain will yield control of Iraq first to an international coalition under the authority of the UN and then, as quickly as is politically feasible, entirely to the Iraqis. While the US and Britain effectively control Iraq, rebuilding it and creating democratic institutions, it is inconsistent to hope that they should succeed in their best purposes and also to urge that they be held to account, in an international court, for waging an unjust war.

If we fought an unjust war, then the intentional killing even of the evil-doers amongst the Iraqis will count (morally) as murder, and the unintended deaths of others will be on our heads, whether those deaths were caused by us or by the Iraqis. The bad consequences of our unjust acts are rightly slated home to us. To see this, consider the following: if you attack someone unjustly, and unintentionally injure or kill an innocent bystander, or if you attack someone unjustly and they unintentionally injure or kill someone to protect themselves, then moral responsibility for the unintended deaths falls on you. This is not true if the attack is just, provided that the unintended deaths are not foreseeable and that you have done all you can to prevent them. The same is true of war. If our attack on Iraq is unjust, then even if the people killed in the Baghdad markets were the victims of failed Iraqi ground-to-air missiles, we are morally accountable. To put the matter bluntly, if you are a coalition soldier in Iraq, then whether or not you should be there will radically affect what can be said in your defence when you shot civilians because you feared they might be suicide bombers or because you could not tell them apart from the Iraqi soldiers who shed their uniforms to mingle undetected amongst the civilians.

Most parts of the UN are, I think, as corrupt and ineffectual as George Bush says. Almost nothing is to be said for the UN except that it is all we have. Why do we need it? Because its demise or marginalisation would undermine the international institutions we need if we are to carry forward the spirit of Nuremberg, institutions that will see justice done to those, like Hussein, who have committed crimes against humanity and to those, like the leaders of the coalition of the willing, who wage war when there is no necessity for it.

II

When the weapons inspectors went to Iraq late in 2002, it was widely predicted that it might take them up to a year to do their job. Just before the war began, the UN chief weapons inspector Hans Blix said that they might be able to do it in six more months. No one can sensibly doubt that Saddam allowed the inspectors to return only because the Americans were serious when they threatened war, but it became clear quite early that the US regretted agreeing to the renewal of UN inspections.

Supporters of the war say that they knew that Saddam

would never fully co-operate. But the question was not whether he would fully co-operate, but whether we had reason to believe that when the weapons inspectors declared their job done he would have sufficient weapons to justify an attack against him. No one can justifiably claim to know the answer to that question. Only a child would have failed to realise at the outset that Saddam would do all he could not to comply with the UN resolution; Bush's arrogant tone made it mandatory if he was to avoid total humiliation. Yet he complied in most respects, grudgingly, minimally, but sufficiently to offer Blix a sober hope that war could be avoided and the authority of the UN enhanced. Blix may have been proved wrong, but those who would not wait to see cannot claim that they went to war only as a last resort.

To tread the path of law one must be patient, resisting temptations to by-pass procedures and the evidence they require because one thinks that one knows in advance who is guilty and for what actions. Inescapably, respect for justice and its embodiment in law makes us vulnerable to those who will do all in their power to make the law and those who defend it look like fools. Ironically, this is a constant theme in Hollywood westerns. If I am right, then the Americans were exasperated not because Saddam was abusing the fact that they had taken the path of international law, but because they regretted taking it. They were impatient for war and, to embellish a little on a point made by Avashai Margalit, even

if Saddam had personally taken the inspectors to sites brist-
ling with weapons of mass destruction, they would have said
that those weapons were merely the tip of the iceberg.

Tony Blair tried hard to persuade the Security Council
to pass a second resolution authorising an attack. Had he
succeeded, the Security Council would have authorised war
before it was necessary. The war would therefore not have
been just, nor even legal, for it would almost certainly have
breached the UN Charter. Far from failing to rise to its
responsibilities, as the leaders of the coalition say, the Security
Council rose well to them, mindful of the conditions for just
and lawful war, and refusing to betray its responsibilities by
succumbing to US bribes and threats. True, it was awakened
to its responsibilities only because the US seemed determined
to go to war. Once awakened, however, it judged—rightly
in my view, but surely at least reasonably—that the inspectors should be given more time. The motives of France,
Germany and Russia were, it is true, more than a little mixed,
but the mixtures were no more disreputable than is usual
in the lives of nations or than they would have been for
many of the smaller nations on the Security Council if
the US had succeeded in bribing or bullying them. Australia's
support of the United States may prove to be in its
security interests, but it is unlikely that they will assist us when
we are made to pay the price of Howard's self-indulgent
hubris in accusing the UN, France and Germany of

dereliction in their duty to the community of nations.

What would it have cost the coalition to grant Blix his six months? Would Saddam and the terrorists who threaten us have taken it as a sign of weakness? Perhaps, but only because the coalition had created a situation which would have made it appear weak. Had it not been so bellicose in its rhetoric, had it not responded with foolish impatience to Saddam's predictable evasions, had it made it clear from the outset that it would follow the path of law, accepting that law needs evidence and time to gather it, then it is unlikely that agreeing to Blix's request for more time would have seemed weak or indecisive.

Defending the timing of the attack, John Howard said it was foolish to think that the Americans could allow their troops to sit indefinitely in the desert. To the extent that that is true, the fault lies again with the coalition, especially with the Americans. Troops should never have been deployed in a way that made it militarily impossible or even seriously difficult to give the inspectors the time they needed, and therefore international law time to do its work. Suppose that is granted. Should we nonetheless accept that, reckless though our strategy may have been, there would have come a time when the approach of summer and the number of troops occupying the desert forced our hand? Not if one seriously believes, as all the leaders of the coalition profess to, that every human life is sacred. If you really believe that, and if you were confronted with someone grieving over the death of even one of the people killed by the coalition, it is hard to know what you could say if you were presenting Howard's case. Could you say that, though you regretted the loss of this life, and indeed of every life, it was really not sensible to ask coalition soldiers to risk boredom and demoralisation by staying in the desert for a further six months, or tax-paying citizens of the countries of the coalition to incur the extra cost of keeping them there, or to encourage suspicion about the coalition's will to fight?

III

On the day when fourteen civilians were killed in a Baghdad market, the world expressed its pain. Over six hundred Iraqi soldiers were reported killed on the same day, yet if one is to judge by newspaper and television commentary, it seemed of little importance. Judging by the attention given to them, the dead soldiers did not matter much to the leaders of the coalition or to most of the media. The same conclusion is suggested by the fact that no serious efforts have been made to estimate the number of dead Iraqi soldiers. We were told that up to 2000 were killed in the first 'incursion' into Baghdad. I have heard that when coalition troops fought against Iraqi conscripts in the north, they bombed on a line parallel to the trenches hoping to terrify the men into flight or surrender. I don't know whether that is true. It is not likely to be true of the softening-up operations against the Republican Guard. At least three divisions—each, we have been told, containing more than 10,000 soldiers—were 'destroyed' or 'degraded' to an extent that rendered them incapable of putting up a serious fight.

People sometimes say there are no rules in war, but that is usually because they want to justify atrocities or because they are so appalled by the carnage that their capacity for judgment has collapsed and they find the application of moral distinctions to war obscene. Clearly, however, there are differences between wars in which belligerents respect one another and wars in which they treat each other with contempt. Those differences show themselves, for example, in the treatment of prisoners, in the treatment of the wounded and in the treatment of the dead. And insofar as we judge how the wounded should be treated, we must also judge the weapons that wound them. To call the generalised expression of such judgments 'rules' is perhaps misleading, for it eases people too quickly into the frame of mind that prompts them to ask: 'Do you think war is a game?'

Twelve years earlier Operation Desert Storm set a chilling precedent for ruthless slaughter. True, the dead were soldiers serving an aggressor, but the distinction between killing aggressors and killing defenders or between killing civilians and killing combatants does not overlap neatly with the distinction between respect for human life and contempt for it. The 'softening-up' operations of Desert Storm that bombed tens of thousands of Iraqi soldiers into the desert sands showed a brutal lack of regard for human life. It is hard to see how one could show such contempt for the humanity of combatants and at the same time show genuine respect for the humanity of civilians by careful (and much publicised) attempts to minimise 'collateral damage'. The same is true of this war. Respect for humanity is not so easily divisible. The frequent attempt to make it so is one of the reasons why George Orwell was scornful of the sometimes hypocritical importance we attach to the distinction between combatants and civilians.

If concern over the killing of enemy civilians is an expression of a sense of common humanity with them, then our sense of a common humanity with enemy soldiers must also show itself in the way that we treat them, when they are alive and also when they are dead. And if that sense of a common humanity is informed by the belief that every human life is sacred—that every human being without exception must be treated as an end in himself and never merely as a means to an end—then it must show itself in the way we treat even those combatants who are guilty of crimes against humanity, as many in the Republican Guard may have been.

Colin Powell, it is reported, was deeply troubled by the extent of the killing that made an obscenity of that aspect of Operation Desert Storm. It was, he said, 'unchivalrous'. Even to one who insists on the stringency of the rules of war, that expression sounds anachronistic. Only when fighting is for the most part face to face does it seem to have living use. It was striking, therefore, that Powell did not realise that the bombing that so disturbed him was not an example of unchivalrous conduct, but an example of a practice that undermined the conditions in which that concept had any serious application.

An analogy might make the point clearer. Propaganda that radically dehumanises the enemy should be seen (I don't know what its legal status is) as a crime against humanity rather than a war crime because it erodes the conditions in which we can retain a sense that shooting enemy prisoners or killing the women and children of the enemy, for example, are war crimes. I suspect that the reason why so many people were troubled by the awesome bombing of Iraqi troops in their bunkers (and perhaps why the leaders of the coalition seemed keen to divert our eyes from it) was not just because it was relentless, or because the casualities must have been very high, but because it made craters in the conceptual space that gives sense to talk of the rules of war. Whether that was because the bombing revealed the battle to be so pitifully unequal, or because it was so brutal, or because it was so impersonal, or some combination of the three, I cannot say. From one perspective, of course, the bombing was just an extension of what artillery barrages brought into the world. Sometimes however, differences of degree become differences of kind.

What is a nation to do if it possesses such technological capacity as the Americans now have? Should it deliberately refrain from using it in war? Should it deliberately expose its troops to enemy fire so battles are more equal? That *would* make war like a game and, in its own way, make it obscene. The answer, I think, is that such weapons should make nations that possess them more rather than less reluctant to go to war. Knowing in advance that it would bomb as it did should have prevented the coalition from going to war when it did, for it went before war was necessary.

As much as an imaginative understanding of what civilians will suffer, an understanding of what such bombing means should enliven our understanding of why war should always be a last resort. Almost certainly, we will pay dearly for what we have done. Such bombing must inflame the hatred in the hearts of those who are alive amongst its victims or those who lost loved ones to it. Denied his ability to fight except impotently in suicidal gestures, our enemy will naturally wish to fight us where he can—in our cities.

IV

If the US had intervened unilaterally in Rwanda, she would now be honoured for redeeming, to some degree, a world that had abandoned the Tutsis to the genocidal ferocity of the Hutus who exterminated them 'like cockroaches'. Instead, the Clinton administration argued, to a UN indecently ready to agree, that the crime against the Tutsis, who were murdered only because they were Tutsis, should not be called genocide. If it were, the US together with all other signatories to the 1948 Convention on the Prevention and Punishment of Genocide, would have been obliged to intervene. Memory of the forsaken Tutsis has haunted argument about whether the world should have intervened on behalf of Saddam's victims. Some people believe that the extent and brutality of his crimes against his people constituted a sufficient justification for the coalition's invasion. Others believe that, though the humanitarian argument (as it came to be called) did not justify going to war, it added weight to other arguments and that, taken as a package, they provided that justification.

Almost everyone now agrees that our failure to intervene militarily in Rwanda shamed us all. Almost no one thinks we should go to war against Zimbabwe even though it is likely that more people will die there than were likely to die in the relatively near future under Saddam. When to intervene is, therefore, a matter of judgment, and decent people will disagree.

There is, I believe, a principle that can guide our thoughts on the matter. Keeping to the spirit of the idea that we should go to war only as a last resort, I would argue that justice permits us to go to war for the sake of those who suffer criminal injustices at the hands of their governments only when, all things considered, we are obliged to do so rather than merely when great good is likely to result from it. Because such an obligation falls upon nations, the effects of its exercise on respect for sovereignty and for international law will be pre-eminent in the list of 'all things considered'.

Sovereignty is not sacred. Sometimes an obligation falls upon any decent nation to attack another sovereign nation for the sake of those against whom the latter commits crimes against humanity. But no one can sanely believe that we are morally bound to attack every nation guilty of that crime, nor even every nation guilty of genocide as defined in the United Nations Convention of 1948. It will always be diffi-cult to justify attacking a nation guilty of those crimes if there are too many other nations guilty of them to much the same degree. Justification will then depend on what can be made of other reasons for going to war. In the context of anything that looks like the present state of international relations, a (moral) obligation to go war exists when our refusal to do so for the sake of the persecuted is rightly seen by them as abandonment—when, in other words, they can justifiably claim that our refusal has wronged them. Rwanda satisfies that criterion. Zimbabwe does not. Neither, I believe, did Iraq. → Why?

If those who are ruthlessly persecuted by their governments can justifiably claim they are wronged by our refusal to wage war on their behalf, then the obligation to go to war falls on us, even though the consequences of doing so are radically uncertain. If, however, we wage war not because we are obliged to but because we want to bring about a great humanitarian benefit so that 'good may come of it', then we must have other reasons that *independently* justify going to war, and we must have good grounds for believing that the aftermath of war will not cause such suffering as to wipe out the benefit. Who can soberly claim to predict the consequences of the war we have just waged?

Nothing I have said explains why I believe that the refusal to attack Iraq would protect us from the accusation, made against us by the victims of the Saddam's regime, that we wronged them by not invading. In fact, I have little to say, beyond suggesting that, with the eyes of the world upon him and with something like the Franco–German proposal in place, Saddam would not have constituted a danger to his people sufficiently different from that constituted by many other dictators. How then could we justify military intervention against him but not against them? But, as I admitted earlier, it is a matter for judgment. My point in saying that I do not believe that the Iraqis could claim they were wronged by our refusal to go to war on their behalf is to introduce a consideration that is often neglected when people weigh up the suffering that would result from intervention against the suffering that would continue in its absence.

Students reading moral philosophy invariably come across examples that ask them to consider whether the murder of an innocent person is justified if it would save the lives of many others. Some students immediately say that the innocent person cannot justifiably be killed because his killing would be murder and we must not murder so that good may come of it or evil be averted by it. Others say, just as promptly, that the person should be killed for it is better that one be killed than (say) ten. In that second group, some say that, since it is right that one person should be killed to save ten, his killing cannot constitute a wrong, or, morally speaking, be an evil; others say that the killing of one is murder and therefore an evil, but a lesser evil than allowing ten others to be killed. Everyone agrees that of two scenarios—one in which there is one person dead, of say, a heart attack, and the other in which ten people are dead for the same reason—the latter is obviously worse.

Thinking about situations of that kind, it has often struck me that none of the ten could claim she was wronged by the refusal to kill the one. Nor could any of them decently ask that another person be killed for her sake. Nor, I believe, could one of them say: not for me taken alone, but for the ten of us taken together. No one has the right to speak on behalf of the others, and no one has the right to make of the others a conglomerate, in which the voice that addresses each individual, asking what she has the right even to hope for, is silenced. Each must ask what she hopes for, and none, I think, can decently hope that another person should be murdered so that her life be spared.

Seen from this perspective, each of the ten finds herself radically individualised. But that, I must now admit, is not a fact of nature. To be radically individuated in that way, for that kind of reason, is not a natural fact that could serve as a universally approved rational basis for moral judgment. It is, rather, the expression of a moral perspective on oneself and one's situation, the perspective Socrates gave voice to when he said that it is better to suffer evil than to do it, and, I think, the perspective from which every individual is taken to be inalienably precious.

Artificial though such examples often are, lessons may sometimes be learnt from them. One is this. Our actions fall under much more complex judgments than is suggested by the maxim that we should always strive to bring about the best state of affairs. There are considerations of justice, and other considerations focussing on what a human life means, whose force does not depend on their contribution to the overall state of affairs, or whether, to simplify a little, people are more benefited in this scenario than in that one. When we consider the consequences of our refusal to act—or better, our realisation that morally we cannot act—it is important always to ask whether those who suffer as a consequence of our incapacity to do what is unjust can say they are wronged.

I believe that they cannot. If we act on their behalf, but unjustly, then the blood of those we kill is on our hands. But if people are killed because we are (morally) compelled to renounce the unjust means that alone could save them, then only their oppressors can be held morally to account.

If we go to war not because we are obliged to but in order to bring about a humanitarian benefit—to save more lives, for example, than we estimate would be lost at our hands because we have intervened—then we must answer the question: 'Who do we think we are—*what* do we think we are—to have taken this upon ourselves?' We must answer that question even if, as is hardly ever the case, we can have reasonable confidence in the consequences of our intervention. What kind of reply can we make to our victims, or to those who mourn them? That it is all for the best? That, all things considered, it is worth it?

Obligations can take the form of necessity. When we are lucidly obliged to go to war we can justifiably say that we will go because it is necessary, a necessity whose moral character is best (if clumsily) expressed with a double negative:

we could not not go. Then, I believe, the question, 'With what right have we taken this upon ourselves?' falls away and with it the language of justification that is characteristic of replies to it. If we are necessitated, we do not have to look at the corpses on one side and the joyfully liberated on the other, or find that the words 'it was worth it' stick to our tongues.

In an existentialist frame of mind, we may suspect that appeals to necessity are always bad faith. But such appeals go deep in our moral experience and are often encountered when it would be silly to suspect that someone was seeking to evade responsibility for their choices. 'What else could I do?' a person replies in response to the question of why she helped an injured person lying by the side of the road, or even, when heroically, she has saved another at great risk to her own life. Such examples show that the necessity of obligation need not be contrasted with compassion. To the contrary, sometimes the truthful claim that one could not turn away from someone in need is the expression of compassion when it is most pure. To elaborate that, however, and to distinguish compassion as a form of moral necessity from compassion—'melting compassion', Kant called it— conceived as a psychological phenomenon, would be the topic of another essay.

I can now reply to those who say the humanitarian argument was not sufficient in itself, but, together with others, constituted a justification for going to war. When it was added to the others, the humanitarian argument did not make going to war a last resort. When the other arguments were added to the humanitarian, they did not turn the passionate desire that the Iraqis should be liberated into an obligation to wage war to ensure that they were. Sometimes a humanitarian crisis can be so severe that military action is at once obligatory and a last resort. Such was the case in Rwanda. But then, of course, the humanitarian argument has no need of others to give it weight.

What are the key distinctions between Iraq and Rwanda?

V

Almost everyone wanted the war to be short despite the boost that an easy victory would give to the US's already overweening arrogance, and the dangers to the world of such arrogance. About halfway through, some people—I was among them—felt, in one part of themselves, such dismay and even disgust at the imbalance of forces, at the ruthless way the Iraqi soldiers were bombed, that they wished, somewhat inchoately, that things were different. Speaking now for myself, reflection soon revealed that wish to be an impossible one, for when it became explicit it became the hope that the Iraqis would put up a better fight. But they could put up a better fight only if they killed more of the coalition's soldiers, some of whom were my fellow Australian citizens and others British soldiers, in whose country and amongst whose people I have lived and worked for more than thirty years. How could I hope that Iraqis might kill Australians and Britons and then live together with the soldiers who returned and with those who would grieve for them if they did not?

Sometimes governments may be so evil that no one who knows what they have done could decently support them. The Nazis created such a government in Germany. For that reason, those Germans who fought against Germany were not only justified in doing so, but could legitimately claim to be the true patriots, fighting so that Germany could once again be a nation that decent people could defend. Clearly, those who were opposed to the war against Iraq could say nothing of the kind.

If one believes that one's country is fighting an unjust war, then one is obliged to protest against that war. Perhaps one may refuse to call the other party to the conflict 'the enemy'. If necessary, one might go to prison rather than be conscripted into such a war. And more besides, of that kind. But one cannot actively support an enemy who is killing one's fellow countrymen and women and at the same time live with them and their loved ones in a form of community whose identity is shaped, in part, by love of and allegiance to a common country. Acknowledgment of that does not censor or even soften the voice of a universal conscience. Rather, in such circumstances, it finds its voice in acknowledgment of the deepening possibilities and constraints of local allegiance. By the same token, local allegiance must answer to the demands of a universal conscience. Often it speaks in the morally individuated voice of a person who insists, against accusations of political naivety or irresponsibility, on the complex interdependencies between her moral and her political identity. If the distinctive use of the first person plural that expresses political fellowship is not modulated, sometimes even radically transformed, by the voice of those who are radically individuated by the demands of morality, then love of country degenerates into its false semblance, jingoism.

The conditions for decent political communality are undermined by radical evil and also by support in wartime for those who would kill one's fellow countrymen and women. They are undermined as surely, if less severely, by those who cry treachery when they sniff out their fellow citizens whose pity for the enemy drives them into inchoate and contradictory wishes of the kind I outlined earlier. Plato would have described those who cry treachery in such circumstances 'troublemakers'. Because they refuse to allow a speaking part to some elements of the soul that may reasonably be in conflict with others, they subvert the possibilities for a just resolution of those conflicts, in the soul and in the community.

VI

Commentators often say that it is hard for anyone who is not American to understand how deeply Americans were shaken by the events of September 11 and how firm they now are in their resolve to do whatever is necessary to prevent another attack. Echoes of this are sometimes heard in Australia in relation to the Bali bombing atrocity. For the most part, the way our leaders have encouraged our resolve does them no credit. It is important to be clear about what they wanted us to do. They wanted us to be prepared to kill tens of thousands of Iraqi soldiers and thousands of Iraqi civilians because, perhaps at some unknown time in the future, a weapon of mass destruction—procured perhaps from Saddam, but more likely from elsewhere—might be used against our cities. Our leaders have also asked us to turn a blind eye, if we cannot give our consent, to the torture of terrorists who may have information about who has, who might be trying to get and who might use such weapons. Alan Dershowitz, the influential Harvard academic lawyer, has argued that a certain degree of torture should be legalised so that we can torture terrorists transparently, without hypocrisy.

Within living memory millions of people have been murdered by tyrants and have died and suffered in wars, but that did not tempt us to defend a doctrine of pre-emption, nor to turn the clock back on the fight to outlaw torture.

When 3000 people were killed in New York, and almost 200 in Bali, John Howard and other national leaders, playing on our fears, urged us to turn the world upside down.

Global terrorism is new, they tell us. It is, but the moral problem it presents to us is as old as thought about morality itself: what are we prepared to do to protect ourselves? Two and a half thousand years after Socrates our leaders urge us, in tones of high moral earnestness, always to be ready to do evil to our enemies before they have much chance of making us suffer it.

If a person fully understood what he was doing, had it vividly before his mind, could he consent to the torture of someone for his sake? Could he plead to grieving Iraqi mothers that he supported the war that killed their children so that he might—just might—be safer because Australian participation in the invasion strengthened its alliance with the world's only superpower? Only someone who lived as though every principle is negotiable when his life is at risk. Such a life is not worthy of a human being. That, I admit, is not a truth written in the heavens. Neither facts nor reason compel its acceptance. But the finest part of our tradition has taught it and many have given their lives rather than betray it. Before democracy, even before freedom, it is this that we should fight for.

I speak for myself. I cannot speak for my fellow citizens. But neither, it is of the utmost importance to remember, can those who would torture terrorists and others for the sake of the hypothetical thousands whose lives may be saved or who, for the same reason, urge us to support pre-emptive wars of the kind we waged against Iraq. Each of us must ask himself whether he can consent to such things—done, it is always said, for the good of the nation to which we belong. We do not, together with others, constitute an indivisible mass for whose collective good evil may be done. No one can rightly say, 'Not for me, but for all the others.' But if, shamelessly in my judgment, we called on our government to protect us, pleading that we are many whereas those we torture are only a few, we could not claim that our government had wronged us if it refused. Nor if it refused to kill thousands of people because their leaders might one day threaten us.

When terrorists were hijacking passenger airliners in the 1970s a close friend, Denis Grundy, insisted that to yield to the demands of terrorists is always to encourage further terrorism. In the fight against terrorism, he argued, each of us should be prepared to die rather than to encourage governments to yield to terrorist demands. We should refuse to plead for our lives when hijackers offer to exchange them for their political demands. To do what he urged we would need even greater courage than was possessed by those brave passengers who crashed their hijacked aeroplane into the fields of Pennsylvania to prevent it from attacking its target, believed to be the Pentagon.

Grundy was right, I believe, and his idea should be extended in ways I have suggested. Volunteers in the 'war against terror' would be prepared to die rather than to plead for their lives when that would encourage further terrorism. They would also refuse to let their government make cowards of them by acting on the assumption that they would support torture and pre-emptive murder in order to save their own skins. Morally, they would then become volunteers in a citizens' army, a quite different kind of 'coalition of the willing'.

WAR AND LIBERATION
Peter Coghlan

As he welcomed home another contingent of Australian troops returning from Iraq on 16 June 2003, John Howard said this: 'We went to war in a just cause, on a proper legal basis, to liberate an oppressed people.'

As commentators like Michelle Grattan and Paul Kelly have noted, this statement is a blatant rewriting of history. The liberation of the Iraqi people from Saddam Hussein's tyranny was not one of the reasons for invading Iraq that the Howard government put before the Australian people in the resolution passed by the House of Representatives on 18 March. The justification for the war in that resolution centred on the threat to 'international peace and security' posed by Iraq's 'continued possession and pursuit of weapons of mass destruction in defiance of its mandatory obligations under numerous resolutions of the UN Security Council'.

Indeed, in his address to the National Press Club on 13 March, the prime minister said, 'I would have to accept that if Iraq had genuinely disarmed, I couldn't justify on its own a military invasion of Iraq to change the regime. I've never advocated that.'

Yet in all his welcome-home speeches to Australian troops, it is precisely regime change for its own sake that John Howard has claimed as the 'just cause' for going to war. Where the liberation of the Iraqi people was once a benefit of disarming Saddam Hussein, it has now become the primary reason for waging war in Iraq.

The reason for this dramatic shifting of the goalposts is obvious. No weapons of mass destruction of the kind that would represent an immediate threat to 'international peace and security' have been found in Iraq. US officials now speak of searching, not for actual weapons, but for evidence of 'weapons programs'. They may find such evidence—though a centrifuge and a set of plans for nuclear bombs buried under a rose bush in a scientist's private garden for twelve years will hardly do. It is true, as Christopher Hitchens argued recently, that Hans Blix would never have found this material. But what the buried centrifuge points to is the success of the UN inspections in containing Saddam Hussein's nuclear ambitions rather than his regime being on the verge of restarting its nuclear weapons program as we were led to believe by George W. Bush and Tony Blair.

Moreover, compelling evidence has now emerged that both the US and British governments pressed ahead with their claims about the certain and imminent threat presented by Iraq's weapons when they knew, or should have known, from their own intelligence agencies that those claims were based on evidence that was ambiguous at best and, in some cases, completely spurious—like the deal for Niger to supply Iraq with uranium. It is now clear, I think, that the US Congress and the British Parliament were misled by their governments about the nature of the threat posed by the Iraqi regime. Both governments should therefore resign.

John Howard has defended his own government's statements in the resolution it put before the House of Representatives on 18 March by saying that our own intelligence services relied on the information provided by the US and British agencies. But that justification will not wash. There can be no graver political issue than the decision to go to war against another nation. The prime minister had a responsibility to ensure that the evidence he was given by foreign intelligence agencies was accurate and trustworthy. Had he checked that evidence carefully, he would have found that it did not support his claim that Iraq's weapons represented an immediate threat to international peace and security. Andrew Wilkie's resignation from the Office of National Assessments in March was a very public acknowledgment of the fact that there were real doubts in the western intelligence agencies about the threat posed by Iraq. John Howard and his government, therefore, should also resign.

Of course, neither Bush, nor Blair, nor Howard will resign. They will continue to defend themselves, as John Howard has done here in Australia, by saying that the war was justified even if no weapons of mass destruction are found. And what made it a just war was the liberation of the Iraqi people from a murderous dictatorship. Actually, that is no justification for their failure to provide their parliaments and their publics with an honest and accurate assessment of Iraq's military capabilities. But it is a clever political ploy—a triumph of spin over truth—because there are many people who now believe, and some who believed before the war began, that the liberation of the Iraqi people was reason enough to invade. Our governments may have misled us, or even lied to us, about Iraq's weapons of mass destruction; but they still did the right thing in overthrowing Saddam Hussein. This is the current of thought that John Howard has openly encouraged.

So what of this humanitarian or liberationist argument for the war on Iraq? Did it, by itself, justify the invasion? One voice that spoke in favour, and spoke with real moral authority, was that of the Foreign Minister of East Timor, Jose Ramos-Horta. In an article entitled, 'War for Peace? It Worked in My Country', printed on 25 February in the *New York Times*, Ramos-Horta began by recalling his two brothers and his sister who were murdered by Indonesian soldiers in the late 1970s and how, terrible as his own family's suffering was, it was only representative of the suffering of his whole country—a country in which there was 'hardly a family…that [had] not lost a loved one'. He went on to note how many western nations, including the US, had contributed to the tragedy of the East Timorese people, just as they had contributed to the tragedy of the Iraqi people, through their military aid to the oppressors or simply through their 'indifference and silence'. But in 1999 those nations 'all redeemed themselves' with the international peacekeeping force that 'helped East Timor secure its independence and protect its people'. The long war of resistance against Indonesian rule, and then the brief but vicious conflict with the Indonesian-backed militia, brought with them 'suffering and misery'. 'It would certainly be a better world,' he said,

> if war were not necessary. Yet I also remember the desperation and anger I felt when the rest of the world chose to ignore the tragedy that was drowning my people. We begged a foreign power to free us from oppression, by force if necessary.

Ramos-Horta's words expressed the humanitarian argument in one of its most powerful forms. His 'desperation and anger' echoes that felt by the Tutsis during the genocide in Rwanda in 1994, or the people of Srebrenica during the ethnic cleansing in 1995. Certainly in each of these last two cases—Rwanda and Srebrenica—the victims expressed a sense of having been abandoned. They felt that the international community had an obligation to protect them from an immediate massacre. And as these massacres unfolded, and then afterwards, there was a widespread feeling in the international community that we had indeed betrayed their victims and that we should have intervened with military force to protect them.

'A (moral) obligation to go to war exists,' Raimond Gaita says, 'when our refusal to do so for the sake of the persecuted is rightly seen by them as abandonment—when, in other words, they can justifiably claim that our refusal has wronged them.' Gaita believes that Rwanda met this criterion, but Iraq did not. Ramos-Horta clearly believes that Iraq did meet the criterion and the invasion of that country was therefore justified on humanitarian grounds alone. Is there any way of determining who is right?

I do not believe there is any simple answer to that question, but I think we can say more about those two crucial qualifying terms in Gaita's formulation: we have an obligation to wage a humanitarian war when our refusal to do so is *rightly* seen by those for whom we are fighting as abandonment and when they can *justifiably* claim that that refusal has wronged them.

It is not hard to discern why the survivors, and, before they were killed, the victims, of Rwanda and Srebrenica could rightly claim to have been abandoned and wronged by the international community. There were two factors at work in both cases. In the first place, there was the obvious and shocking fact of mass murder—the murder of up to 8000 men and boys by the Serb militia forces of Ratko Mladic in Srebrenica, and the murder of up to 800,000 Tutsi men, women and children by Hutu militia in Rwanda.

In the second place, there was the fact that UN forces were present both before and during the massacres—forces that might have prevented the bloodletting had they been given the necessary support. In Rwanda, General Romeo Dallaire, the commander of the UN contingent charged with ensuring peace, warned his superiors in writing of the impending slaughter and asked for reinforcements to contain the Hutu militia. In Dallaire's view, a force of only 5000 experienced soldiers would have been enough to deter the Hutus. His warnings and requests for support went unheeded at the UN and in the major western nations.

In Srebrenica there were 110 Dutch troops guarding the town that the UN had designated a 'safe haven'. Of course the Dutch would have been no match for Mladic's militia had they tried to resist them. In any case, the Dutch were not prepared to confront Mladic and protect the local Muslims as Dallaire's men in Rwanda were prepared to confront the Hutus. But the Dutch soldiers were not given any support that might have stiffened their resolve. The Dutch cabinet took fright and ordered their troops to withdraw leaving the Muslims to Mladic's thugs. The 2002 report on the incident from the Netherlands Institute for War Documentation ('Srebrenica: a "Safe" Area') condemned the cowardice of

Prime Minister Wim Kok's cabinet. In the face of this scathing report, Kok and his government took the only honourable step open to them—they resigned.

We can contrast Rwanda and Srebrenica immediately with the situation in Tibet or Burma or Chechnya. We know that there has been terrible persecution, including incidents of mass murder, of the Tibetan people by the Chinese, of the Burmese hill tribes on the border with Thailand, especially the Karen, by the military rulers of Burma, and of the Chechens by the Russians. And it may well be that the victims of these persecutions feel abandoned by the international community.

None of these cases, however, is directly parallel to Rwanda and Srebrenica. There have not been any UN forces on the ground in these troubled countries to witness the demolition of homes and religious centres, the rapes and the torture and the massacres, and to alert the world to what is happening. We usually hear of the atrocities after the event. The victims of these horrors have not been able to say to us: 'You were there for our protection. You saw what was done to us. You could have intervened to prevent it. And yet you did nothing.' They may be right to feel abandoned if by that we mean that the world has forgotten their plight, or is simply indifferent to it even when it does hear of it. But they would not be justified in claiming that we have abandoned them in the sense of betraying them in the way that we betrayed the Tutsis or the Muslims of Srebrenica. They can justifiably challenge us to put as much diplomatic, moral, and perhaps even economic pressure as we can on their governments to end their oppression. But they cannot say that we have an obligation to wage war on their behalf against their persecutors because our refusal to do so would constitute a betrayal.

Is Iraq like Rwanda and Srebrenica? Some, like Christopher Hitchens, have argued that it is—or, at least, that it is close enough for the case to be morally compelling. The US, Hitchens believes, incurred an obligation to liberate the Iraqi people from Saddam Hussein's tyranny in 1991 at the end of the Gulf War when George Bush Senior betrayed the Shiites and the Kurds by encouraging them to rebel and then abandoning them to Saddam's brutal repression—a repression that led to the murder of perhaps 300,000 people. The Allied forces may not have been in Iraq itself witnessing the massacres as they happened. But they were just next door in Kuwait and they knew of the desperate pleas of the Shiites of the south begging them for help as Saddam's Republican Guard stormed their towns and villages. The obligation to intervene lies here.

For Hitchens, the invasion of Iraq and the overthrow of Saddam are the fulfilment of that obligation twelve years late. And although there were no mass murders taking place at the time of the recent invasion, the Shiites of the south, in particular, continued to suffer under Saddam's terror. The draining of the southern wetlands from 1992 onwards—wetlands that were an integral part of the ancient culture of the Marsh Arabs—is but one example of that continuing terror.

It is true that towards the end of the Gulf War George Bush Senior publicly said this: 'There's another way for the bloodshed to stop, and that is for the Iraqi military and the Iraqi people to take matters into their own hands and force Saddam Hussein, the dictator, to step aside, and then comply with the United Nations resolutions.' The Shiites and Kurds of Iraq took this, and similar statements, to be a sign that Bush would support them in an uprising against Saddam.

But Bush has always denied that he promised the Shiites and Kurds any support—especially any military support that involved US troops invading Iraq. And there is at least one good reason to believe him in this. The Bush administration made it perfectly clear before the war that its goal was limited to driving the Iraqi forces out of Kuwait. The idea of an invasion to overthrow Saddam Hussein was explicitly ruled out. It was on that understanding that Bush was able to gather a coalition of, not three or four as in the coalition of the willing, but some thirty-six nations willing to contribute to the war effort; and it was on that understanding that he was able, unlike Bush junior and Tony Blair, to gain UN Security Council approval for the use of military force to liberate Kuwait.

In the light of his commitment not to invade Iraq, it was folly for Bush Senior to encourage the Shiites to rebel when he knew that he could not help them with troops on the ground. Perhaps, as many argued at the time, the coalition forces could have used their air superiority to drive the Republican Guard units out of Southern Iraq and then to maintain an exclusion zone in which the Shiites could have established some relative autonomy as the Kurds in the north finally did.

But the commitment not to invade, publicly made and endorsed by the UN, does make the claim that Bush Senior and his coalition forces betrayed the Shiites at least a debatable one. Iraq, then, was not like Rwanda and Srebrenica on this score. It did not generate the same clear-cut and overwhelming obligation to intervene militarily to protect the victims of persecution as those cases did.

There is, however, another way of putting the argument that the invasion of Iraq was justified on humanitarian grounds. Recall Ramos-Horta's words about his desperation and anger. He implies that, just as the international community ignored the oppression of the East Timorese for over twenty years after Indonesia annexed their country by force in 1976, and then redeemed itself with the UN military intervention in 1999, so, too, the world ignored the oppression of the Iraqi people for over twenty years until George W. Bush decided to wage war to liberate them from Saddam Hussein.

This way of putting the argument does not rest on the notion of betrayal—though Ramos-Horta has every right to feel that his own people were betrayed by the west, including Australia, when the international community turned a blind eye to the Indonesian invasion of his country. It rests simply on the claim to a common humanity: 'We begged a foreign power to free us from oppression, by force if necessary.' Does this claim generate an obligation in the way that our betrayal of the Tutsis in Rwanda and the Muslims in Srebrenica did?

I think it may. Think of Cambodia (or Kampuchea as it was known then) under Pol Pot from 1975 to 1979 before the Vietnamese invaded and overthrew the Khmer Rouge regime. There are complications here, I know, in the fact that the horrendous US carpet bombing of Cambodia that began in 1969, and for which Henry Kissinger may yet face charges of war crimes, was partly responsible for the rise of the Khmer Rouge. But if we just focus on the period when Pol Pot was in power, we can imagine the people of Cambodia saying to us, as some who escaped the Killing Fields did say to us, something like this: 'We know that you are not responsible for what the Khmer Rouge are doing. We know that none of your representatives are here as peacekeepers and moral witnesses to what is happening to us. But the simple truth is that we are living at the extreme point of human endurance and affliction. And we cry out to you in the name of our common humanity to intervene to save us.'

Sometimes it may be morally impossible to reject this kind of appeal. Can we stand by and watch as the citizens of an entire nation are treated as raw material in an insane and fanatical drive to create a new form of society—indeed, in the perverted minds of the Khmer Rouge, a new form of human being? Can we stand by and watch evil on such a terrifying scale? But that is what we did; and that perhaps is why many in the west felt shamed when it was the communists of Vietnam, our former enemies, who finally put an end to that evil.

In a case like this, the victims of such horrors cannot rightly say that we *betrayed* them by not intervening on their behalf. But they can justifiably say that we *failed* them—that we could have protected them when they had been driven by their persecutors to the very margin of human existence but did not. It is that just claim which may generate an obligation to go to war on their behalf. That obligation falls in the first instance on the community of nations in the UN. But if the UN fails in its duty, then the obligation falls on any group of nations, or any single nation, which has the capacity to help through armed intervention.

Yet there are surely limits to such claims and the obligations they generate. What of the people of the Ukraine in the period from 1932 to 1933 when Stalin deliberately engineered a famine to break their spirit—a famine that cost seven million lives? Assume that we had accurate information about the extent of the horror. Would the Ukrainians have had a just claim on us to wage war on their behalf?

I think the answer has to be no. The reason is clear. The west could not have intervened on behalf of the Ukrainians without precipitating a conflict with the Red Army; and the outcome of the conflict could not have been predicted. A defeat at the hands of the Red Army would have been a real possibility. Then we would have lost on both counts: our forces would have suffered terrible casualties and we would have failed the Ukrainians anyway.

So, here, the radical uncertainty that often attends on humanitarian military intervention does make a difference to our moral judgment. We might have had a reasonable hope of success in protecting the Cambodians had we chosen to invade that country during Pol Pot's rule. But when we are faced with a major military power, our chances of success are obviously weakened. In the nuclear age, they may be weakened to the point where we cannot act without precipitating a conflagration involving the deaths of many millions. That is why, to return to two earlier cases, we would be justified in refusing any cries for military intervention—cries made in the name of our common humanity—of the Chechens and the Tibetans.

(I will not pursue here the question of whether the possibility of precipitating a nuclear war even sets a limit in those cases where we will betray a people if we refuse to intervene. I am inclined to think we are obliged to stand by those we have already made a commitment to and stare down the threat of nuclear retaliation.)

For all the talk of Iraq's reconstituted nuclear weapons program, it was clear before the invasion by the coalition of the willing that Iraq's military would be no match for the US war machine. There were differences over how long the war would last. But there was no doubt the Iraqi army would be defeated. So did the suffering of the Iraqi people under Saddam Hussein constitute the same kind of claim on us as that of the Cambodian people under Pol Pot?

I do not think there is any question that the great mass of Iraqi people were brutalised and terrorised by Saddam's police state. This was vividly caught in a conversation Euan Ferguson of the *Observer* had in early June 2003 with a poet by the name of Abed al Kareem who was an inmate of al Rashad Psychiatric Hospital in Baghdad. Ferguson asked Kareem if he blamed the Americans for the looting that was taking place, including the looting in the hospital in which he lived. Kareem replied:

> You must remember how much we hated Saddam, how happy we are that he is gone. Saddam not only damaged us physically, but he damaged the…the grain of ourselves. So much that was good and beautiful about the Iraqi people. There

was no culture, no teaching, and he turned humans into animals, which is what you see in the streets of Baghdad. This is not true Iraqi people. These are people made mad by Saddam.

Iraq was truly a country 'drowning', to use Ramos-Horta's word, in the evil inflicted on it by Saddam Hussein and his corrupt sons.

Yet Cambodia under Pol Pot was in another category again. This was a whole nation *in extremis*—a people reduced to living in the kind of hellish conditions that Antony Beevor describes in *Stalingrad*. That is why the cries for help of the Cambodian people made an immediate and compelling claim on our common humanity.

The stark truth is that there are many countries like Iraq, and many peoples who are living under oppression and persecution, terrorised and brutalised by the apparatus of the police state—and subject every now and then to mass murder. Zimbabwe, as most people know, is drowning under Robert Mugabe; North Korea, as most know, is drowning under Kim Jong-Il; Burma, as many know, is drowning under its generals; and Turkmenistan, as a few know, is drowning under Saparmurad Niyazov who is almost as cruel and piti-less a dictator as Saddam.

The peoples of all these nations—and more—could lay claim in the name of our common humanity to our military intervention to liberate them. And, in every case except perhaps that of North Korea, we would have reasonable grounds for thinking that our intervention would be successful. I have argued that those claims would not be as compelling as that of the Cambodians under Pol Pot. And the international community simply does not have the resources to tackle all of these cases.

So deciding which cases demand an armed response is a matter of judgment. Typically that judgment is determined by other factors besides humanitarian concerns. Australia took a leading role in the UN military intervention to free the East Timorese people because of our strategic interest in the peace and order of the countries to our immediate north. John Howard's commitment to military support for the government of the Solomon Islands explicitly follows this logic. We are concerned for the suffering of the local people who have been subject to continuing clashes between rival gangs and to the oppression of a corrupt police force. At the same time, we wish to avoid a 'failed state' that could become a breeding-ground for crime and terrorism in our region. At least that is the theory. The chest-beating rhetoric of John Howard and Alexander Downer about being 'tough', and 'doing the job', and not needing UN approval, may yet undermine our humanitarian concern and cast us in the role of colonial masters setting the incompetent natives to rights.

There are, however, several other considerations that we

must take into account in deciding whether a particular humanitarian intervention is justified when there is no clear and compelling obligation laid on us to go to war. I will discuss five such considerations in the light of the invasion of Iraq.

The first is obvious, a standard part of traditional Just War Theory. We must ask ourselves whether we have exhausted all other attempts to modify the behaviour of the oppressive regime and whether our decision to wage war is truly a last resort. I do not think that the invasion of Iraq was a last resort in relation to the disarming of Saddam Hussein. I think there were signs that Hans Blix was having some success in uncovering prohibited weapons such as the long-range missiles his inspectors destroyed just prior to the war.

But in relation to Saddam's oppression of his own people, we should be under no illusions. He cynically exploited the suffering inflicted on ordinary Iraqis during the long period of sanctions by allowing his cronies to control sections of the Food for Oil program and to enrich themselves in the thriving black market. Moreover, he used the sanctions program to blame the US—the main enforcer of the military blockade—for the many shortages his nation laboured under. If he was to be removed, it was clear that it would only be through external force of arms.

The second consideration is this. Since the kind of case we are now dealing with involves judgment rather than an overwhelming sense of moral necessity, it is usually preferable if the armed intervention is undertaken by the UN, or by a broad coalition of nations. The discussion required to achieve consensus in the UN, or to draw together a broad coalition, provides a brake on the arbitrariness that may characterise the judgment of individual nations. When a single nation that takes the lead in building a coalition to liberate a persecuted people fails to convince other nations to join it, as the US failed so conspicuously to do with the invasion of Iraq, it does not automatically mean that its humanitarian objective is misguided. But it is surely a worrying sign which should make that nation think again.

The US did not think again. Rather, it sought to bribe and bully the smaller nations on the UN Security Council into supporting its relentless determination to invade Iraq.

The third consideration concerns the attitudes of the people we are seeking to help. In any decision to go to war to liberate a nation from oppression, we must be sure that the victims of that oppression really want our intervention. If, for example, there was a widespread view amongst a perse-cuted people that having foreign troops in their homeland would be humiliating, and that they would prefer to try to overthrow their oppressive regime by themselves, then any intervention on our part would wrong them and serve only to compound their suffering.

Alternatively, the persecuted people might be desperate

for intervention on their behalf, but only on terms that enabled them to maintain their sense of national pride and dignity. So they might want the intervention to be conducted essentially by countries with which they have a cultural affinity. They might reject that intervention if it was to be undertaken or led by a particular nation whose culture they were ill at ease with.

Both of these elements were at work in Iraq. Many Iraqis rejoiced at Saddam's demise. Yet many were also shamed that they could not overthrow him themselves. As one Iraqi woman, a doctor in Baghdad, put it: 'Saddam was an unjust ruler, but maybe one day we could have got rid of him and not had these foreigners come.'

And 'these foreigners' were not just any invaders. They were the British, the former colonial rulers of Iraq; and they were the Americans, the bearers, in the eyes of many Iraqis, of a base hedonistic culture, and the protectors of Israel against the just demands of the Palestinian people. To have to be liberated was shameful enough; to have to be liberated by Britons and Americans, especially Americans, was doubly humiliating. I am sure the editor of *Gulf News*, Abdul Haid Ahmad, spoke for many Iraqis when he wrote, on the morning after Baghdad fell, that although he was glad the Iraqi people were now free of Saddam, it was nonetheless 'a heart-breaking moment for any Arab—seeing marines roaming the streets of Baghdad, the capital of the Caliph al Rashid, the city that presented to the world sciences, literature, art and philosophical thought during the reign of the glorious Abbasid Empire.'

I do not think that these points tell decisively by themselves against the humanitarian argument. After all, the Iraqis still welcomed the destruction of Saddam's regime, however that was achieved. But when coupled in particular with the issue of motive and intention, which I will come to shortly, these points become more potent.

The fourth consideration centres on the question of who we will be waging war against in any armed humanitarian intervention where no overwhelming obligation falls on us. If the only people who are likely to resist us are the agents of the persecution that we are seeking to end, there is no moral problem. These will often be special forces chosen for their loyalty to their political leaders. They will be guilty of terrible crimes, often including crimes against humanity, and so legitimate targets of our armed forces.

It may, however, be possible that the resistance we face in invading another country will come mainly from members of the regular armed services. These people may not be guilty of any crimes. They will often be conscripts or individuals who have joined the military because it provides a steady job in a society where regular work may be difficult to find. Some of these soldiers may fight because they are ordered to do so. Others may fight because they honestly believe that they are defending their homeland against a foreign invader. As members of their nation's armed forces, sworn to defend their country, they may find the prospect of being invaded by foreign powers shameful and humiliating.

Do we wrong such individuals when we attack and kill them in the course of an intervention to liberate their nation from oppression? I think this is a real and significant issue. It is not an issue that arises in those cases where we act out of moral necessity like Rwanda, Srebrenica or Cambodia. It would have been impossible for Mladic's men, or the Khmer Rouge soldiers, not to be aware of the horrors their leaders were inflicting on others. Those horrors were taking place around them at the hands of their own comrades even if they themselves were not directly involved. They could not have resisted a humanitarian invader and justly claimed that they were only defending their homeland.

In the case of Iraq, it would not have been possible for an ordinary Iraqi soldier to be unaware of the daily injustices of Saddam's police state—the bribery and corruption, the random beatings, the false imprisonment and the torture in the police stations and the prisons. But it was surely possible for an ordinary Iraqi soldier from the Sunni region in central Iraq not to know of, or at least not to know the full extent of, Saddam's worst crimes in the past, like the gassings in Kurdistan in the early 1980s and the massacres of the Shiites in the South in 1991. Or they may have known of these crimes against humanity but believed that they were in the past and that the regime, though still oppressive, no longer inflicted that kind of evil on its citizens. (They may not have known of the ongoing destruction of the culture of the Marsh Arabs or they may have accepted Saddam's propaganda that the draining of the wetlands was in Iraq's economic interest.)

These were the men, regular army soldiers rather than members of the Saddam Fedayeen or the Republican Guard, who were killed in large numbers by the forces of the coalition of the willing. Media correspondents saw hundreds of their bodies lying beside their burnt-out vehicles along the 500-kilometre highway from the Jordanian border to Baghdad. We do not know the exact numbers because, scandalously, their remains were never counted. Jonathan Steele from the *Guardian*, extrapolating from the numbers of dead troops he counted around Baghdad, estimates that the final toll of Iraqi military dead is anywhere between 13,500 and 45,000.

How should we regard the regular troops of an oppressive state? If we see the bulk of them as frightened conscripts compelled to fight, we might hope that they will desert or surrender at the first opportunity. That was clearly the US expectation in Iraq. We may have to attack and kill some of these men. Their deaths would be a tragic necessity to be regretted and mourned in much the same way that we regret and mourn the loss of civilians unintentionally killed in the conflict.

But if we have reason to believe that a reasonable number of regular troops are likely to fight in defence of their nation, we face a dilemma. On the one hand, we can see them as unwitting defenders of a hateful and murderous regime. When we do that, they may become legitimate targets of our humanitarian intervention. On the other hand, we can see them as legitimate defenders of their nation against our aggression. When we do that, we cannot attack and kill them without wronging them.

The question turns on whether we judge that the regular soldiers can in good conscience acknowledge the crimes committed by their government against its own people and yet still believe themselves to be justified in resisting a foreign invasion—even one that aims to liberate them from their oppressive state. If we think that this is a real possibility, then I do not see how, in justice, we can proceed with an armed intervention.

The difficulty here, of course, is determining whether this possibility is a real one. Sometimes it may be clear that the regular soldiers will not resist but will lay down their arms. Perhaps we have been in communication with their commanders and they have convinced us that that is the situation. But in other cases, we may simply not know, or we may suspect that many of the regular troops will resist. Then, I think, we are morally bound to proceed with the greatest caution.

Iraq, in my view, was such a case. While we knew before the war that the Republican Guard were to be the mainstay of the defence of Baghdad, we also knew that regular Iraqi forces were being deployed throughout the country; and while the US conducted an intense campaign to persuade these regular forces to desert, there was no indication that they would do so. In these circumstances, the coalition of the willing was obliged to reconsider its plans for an invasion.

The fifth and final consideration is the question of motive—or, in the language of traditional Just War Theory, 'right intention'. Sometimes a humanitarian concern for a persecuted people can be more or less pure and disinterested. The belated dispatch of UN reinforcements to Rwanda was born of international outrage at the slaughter and shame that we had not acted sooner. But most interventions to liberate a persecuted people are undertaken for self-interested strategic reasons as well as humanitarian concerns. These motives need not conflict. In the case of East Timor, Australia's interest in stability and peace in the region to our immediate north coincided with our compassion for the suffering of the East Timorese people and our anger at the wrongs inflicted on them by the Indonesian-backed militia.

Was there a similar coincidence of motive in the invasion of Iraq? Bush, Blair and Howard would have us believe so. But I think the answer to that question must be an emphatic no.

We now know from Paul Wolfowitz's notorious admission in *Vanity Fair* that the US administration settled on weapons of mass destruction as the *casus belli* for 'bureaucratic reasons…because it was the one reason everyone could agree on.' What, then, were the other reasons? In my view, Thomas Friedman of the *New York Times* nailed those reasons on 4 June 2003 in an article entitled 'Because We Could'.

The first reason for the invasion, Friedman argued, was simply that 'after September 11 America needed to hit someone in the Arab–Muslim world…because a terrorism bubble had built up over there…that posed a real threat to the open societies of the West and needed to be punctured'. The US hit Saddam 'because it could…because he deserved it and because he was right in the heart of that world'. Second, according to Friedman, the US went to war 'to help build a decent Iraq as a model for others' in the region thus further 'defusing the ideas of mass destruction which are really what threaten us'. And, finally, there was the humanitarian reason: 'Saddam's regime was an engine of mass destruction…and needed to be stopped.'

The extraordinary thing about this article is that Friedman does not see how the first and second reasons undermine and corrupt the third. The first reason, the need to 'hit someone in the Arab–Muslim world' so as to puncture the 'terrorism bubble', is the motivation of the bully. It is punitive and vengeful. It says to the Arab world: 'Look, this is what our military power can do. You challenge us at your peril.' It is the motivation that goes with George W. Bush landing on the deck of the USS *Abraham Lincoln* in combat clothing and declaring to the cheering sailors that the hostilities in Iraq were at an end due to the power and the glory of the American military forces. And it is the motivation that goes with Bush's swaggering taunt to the Iraqis engaged in guerrilla attacks on the occupying US troops, a taunt straight out of an Arnold Schwarzenegger or Sylvester Stallone film—'Bring them on.'

Are we seriously to believe that thousands of innocent Iraqi civilians and regular soldiers were killed for this? It is a motive that is utterly at odds with compassion for the Iraqi people and it makes a mockery of the goal of liberating them from oppression. It is a motive that corrupts any humanitarian concern.

The second reason Friedman cites—reconstructing Iraq as, in George W. Bush's own words, 'a dramatic and inspiring example of freedom for other nations in the region'—does not contradict the humanitarian motive in principle. No one would want to see Iraq descend into the tribal conflict that once again bedevils Afghanistan, or succumb to the cruel power of another dictator, or be forced to live under the religious tyranny of fanatics like the Taliban.

But while the Bush administration says that it will allow the Iraqis to choose their own form of government, its key spokesmen have made it abundantly clear that the kind of freedom they envisage for Iraq is the American version of freedom—the freedom of a secular capitalist state. So we get this from Donald Rumsfeld: 'If you're [asking] how would we feel about an Iranian-type government with a few clerics running everything in the country, the answer is: That isn't going to happen.' This is simply the brutal application of the kind of arrogance and self-righteousness expressed in the declaration George W. Bush will perhaps be most remembered for: 'The liberty we prize is not America's gift to the world, it is God's gift to humanity.' Yes, but God gave it to America first, apparently; and now America, with God's blessing, is passing it on, by force if necessary, to Iraq and then to whole Arab–Muslim world.

But if we are genuinely moved by compassion for the Iraqi people, we cannot prescribe for them in advance how church and state should be related in their new community. In the eyes of many Muslims, the separation of church and state in the west has led to godless and sinful societies where the dominant values are profane ones—the crass and selfish search for material wealth and sensual pleasure. American society, with its sexual explicitness in advertising and the media, and with its brazen wealth amidst widespread poverty, seems especially abhorrent from this point of view. The US may have some elements of freedom: Iraqis, like any other people, can appreciate the fact that some of the very

American journals that supported the war, like the *New Republic*, are now openly and courageously exposing the Bush administration's manipulation of the intelligence assessments of Saddam's weapons of mass destruction. Here is American democracy at its best. But where is America's equality and fraternity? At this point the issue of motivation overlaps with the question of humiliation. To be told by Americans, of all people, how they should govern themselves is especially galling to many deeply religious Iraqis.

So it came as no surprise when Iraq's leading Shia cleric, Ayatollah Ali Sistani, issued a *fatwa* condemning Paul Bremer's plans to appoint rather than elect the Governing Council that will draft a new constitution. Sistani himself does not want an Iranian theocracy in Iraq. But he does want Islam to be at the centre of Iraqi national life—as this comment in his *fatwa* indicates:

> There is no guarantee that this council would grant a constitution that accorded with the highest interests of the Iraqi people and would express their national identity, among the pillars of which is the foundation of the pure religion of Islam and its noble social virtues.

A genuine humanitarian concern for the Iraqi people would not involve the kind of condescension, and sometimes outright contempt, that is evident in the US reconstruction program. In fact, if the US was genuinely moved by compassion for the Iraqis, it would have already recognised that America is not the nation best placed to take the lead in helping Iraqis rebuild their country. It would have acknowledged how it is perceived by Arab Muslims and invited other nations more in sympathy with Arab sensibilities to join it in the reconstruction effort. Or it would have simply passed control of that effort much more rapidly to the Iraqis themselves than it did in the first few months after the war.

But that is exactly the problem. The Bush administration could not do either of these things because its goal of remaking Iraq as a symbol of freedom in the Arab–Muslim world was flawed from the start. It was always and essentially a remaking of Iraq in its own image.

So, here too, the self-interested motive corrupts the humanitarian motive. Some commentators have claimed that this does not matter. They argue that the Americans did a good thing in ousting Saddam and liberating the Iraqi people even if some of their motives were base. Consider, they say, a policeman who kills a violent escaped convict who has taken a number of hostages and is threatening them. The policeman does well even if his motive is to play the hero and gain the admiration of his fellow officers and the public at large.

This analogy works up to a point. If the policeman performs his duties conscientiously, his vanity will be channelled into actions that serve the common good. He will act in our interest as well as in his own. But if, driven by his desire to play the hero, he spurns normal police procedures and recklessly attacks the convict, firing wildly and killing one or two hostages along with his intended target, would we still insist that he did the right thing? I think not. Now his vanity will be seen as having perverted his sense of social responsibility as a policeman. The very act of ending the convict's violent rampage and freeing the hostages will have been corrupted.

We can see the same thing happening in the way the US forces conducted the war. It is a standard principle of Just War Theory that an armed conflict must not involve deliberate attacks on civilians and must try to avoid harming them even when that harm is unintentional. We would expect a nation that goes to war to liberate a persecuted people to be especially conscious of this principle.

Although serious questions have been raised about its use of cluster bombs, the coalition of the willing did seem to take special care to avoid civilian casualties in its air campaign. However, evidence is now emerging from journalists like Peter Beaumont and Ed Vulliamy of the *Observer* (22 June and 6 July), that the US ground forces did not exercise the same care in their operations. They appear to have fired on any vehicle that approached them on their path to Baghdad. As a consequence, many civilians, including men, women and children in the Shia areas, were killed and injured in their private cars and in public buses as they tried to escape the fighting.

No doubt the American ground troops feared being attacked by the Fedayeen masquerading as civilians. But the indiscriminate nature of their fire was also due to the ruling spirit they had taken over from their President. They were not there to fight out of compassion for a long-suffering and abused people. They were there, as one soldier put it, 'to kick some ass'. The result, according to Beaumont, was a 'recklessness and a lack of care for civilian casualties that borders on the criminal'.

We can see the same perversion of the humanitarian motive even more clearly in the shameful failure of the Bush administration to anticipate the chaos that would follow the overthrow of Saddam's regime and to respond to it quickly and decisively. Again, this can partly be explained by the surprising speed of the fall of Baghdad. But an army and an administration moved by a desire to liberate a people could not have stood by, as the US forces stood by, and watched as building after building, including hospitals and major cultural centres that had been designated for protection before the war, was looted and torched. Abdul Karim Anwar Obeid, the General Manager of the Department of Religious Affairs, saw his ministry building set ablaze. Afterwards, as he sifted through the ashes of the irreplaceable collection of copies of the Koran that the building had housed, some of them over a thousand years old, he remarked: 'When Baghdad fell to the Mongols in 1258, these books survived. This time they didn't.'

In the face of the looting, Donald Rumsfeld was arrogantly dismissive. 'Stuff happens,' he said. His words summed up the American attitude. There was no protest from either the Blair or Howard governments.

The coalition of the willing may have overthrown Saddam Hussein and his Baath Party thugs. No one could do anything other than rejoice at that. But the coalition has not liberated the Iraqi people. It may yet redeem itself as the west, in Ramos-Horta's view, redeemed itself in East Timor. Or it may be saved, not by its own doing, but by the fact that large sections of the Shia community remain patient and co-operative despite the chaos and the humiliation they now suffer. But I think the crowds that gathered on the streets of Baghdad within days of the fall of the city knew what they were about when they chanted, 'La Amreeka, La Saddam'— 'No to America, No to Saddam.'

So was the invasion justified on humanitarian grounds alone? I respect the Ramos-Hortas of the world who argued the case for armed intervention to liberate the Iraqi people. But I think their view was tragically mistaken. The invasion and occupation of Iraq was, and is, essentially an aggressive and unjust act of war.

ARMS AND HUMANITY
Guy Rundle

> I have never seen a situation so bad that the arrival
> of a policeman cannot make it worse.
>
> Brendan Behan

Halfway through the largest of the anti-war marches in Melbourne in the weeks prior to the invasion of Iraq, I dropped out of the head of the crowd and took a perch near the corner of Swanston and Collins streets to watch the people surge by. I have been on many marches for many causes in years past, and I have seen long crowds take a long time to pour past. But none like this. There seemed to be an inexhaustible supply of human beings, coming for ever.

Successive state governments have done their best to deprive Victorians of a genuine public square in which to assemble, and so the people began to back up from the soon-filled space in Federation Square. Eventually the march poured back into itself, so that it filled the streets of the whole lower part of the city. The mood was jubilant, positive, energetic, but also marked with foreboding about what was about to occur. Many people thought that the global mass human presence that weekend—about eight million people across the cities of the world—marked the emergence of 'a new superpower', that of the people, and that such mass action would lead to an abandonment of war preparations.

Six weeks or so after the war I wondered what many of the participants in that march were thinking. The polls showed that the high number of Australians opposed to participation in a unilateral US-led coalition invasion of Iraq had begun to shrink as soon as the conflict began. By the middle weeks of the war, a majority had now swung round either in favour of it, or at the very least to a position that they 'supported our troops'. Weeks after the conflict had officially finished, when a number of mass graves had begun to be dug up, that support stayed high, despite the continued non-appearance of weapons of mass destruction. Pro-war commentators across the world took the opportunity to lambast the anti-war movement for its 'pacifism' and alleged lack of concern for the Iraqi population. A number of commentators who had opposed the conflict, such as the playwright Joanna Murray-Smith, were happy to give the public *mea culpa* demanded. The dominant feeling abroad was one of confusion and doubt. Did we do the right thing? Were we simply acquiescing in the face of tyranny?

Now the situation and dominant mood have changed yet again. Because Australian troops are no longer involved in Iraq, and because the Bali bombing trials have occurred in the interim, attention has shifted away. It is now almost universally accepted that no weapons of mass destruction will be found, and widely accepted that they were destroyed or disposed of years ago. Yet the continued turmoil in the country—about as many US troops have been killed following the declaration that the conflict was concluded as during it, and a large number of Iraqi civilians have also died—has taken the gloss off. Should the situation develop into broader revolt against US forces, and/or civil war, the confusion will grow further.

Nothing could indicate this unstable mood—about war, peace, and how the decision was made—more exactly than the findings of polls taken in the wake of revelations that the assertion that Saddam Hussein had been trying to buy uranium from Niger was false, and was known to be false by US and Australian intelligence agencies. More than two-thirds of those polled believed John Howard had misled the Australian public; yet the same number also believed he had taken the right course of action in the war. This would seem to indicate that a significant number of people are willing to surrender any demand that the government should have presented the facts honestly in making its case for war—as if the result of the war has abashed them into silence or disengagement.

This is especially true among the many groups and social movements who are identified, by themselves or others, to be of the 'left'. In Australia, the left was almost wholly opposed to the war from the start, and throughout; in the US, and especially in the UK, there was a more fundamental split with a number of high-profile figures—Christopher Hitchens perhaps the most prominent—excoriating former comrades for refusing to join a popular front in a war against an enemy no less fascist than those struggled against in World War II. Those on the left who had maintained an anti-war stance out of pure horror at the conduct of full-scale war were thus likely to find its rapid conclusion and relatively— and that word should be emphasised—low casualties all the more challenging to their deeply held beliefs, especially as the full horrors of Saddam Hussein's regime became known.

For those who still see themselves as of the left—for the oppressed against the oppressor—across the globe, the challenges of the right, of 'popular front' leftists like Christopher Hitchens and of more idiosyncratic pro-war statements that came from old radical leftists such as Albert Langer, are worth taking seriously. In an era in which the world is dominated by a single superpower, the question of unilateral intervention will come up more frequently, and with a greater possibility of being answered in the affirmative. Barely before the Australian Iraq force had touched back down at home, we were on a mission to restabilise the Solomon Islands, which would itself lead to the creation of a 'Pacific Union', under Australian 'protection'. In Africa, the Americans, already overstretched in Iraq and elsewhere, have played a waiting game and eventually committed troops to Liberia. On the other hand, far worse tyrannies and atrocities—Burma, North Korea, the Russians in Chechnya, the continued strife in the Congo region—go unattended.

Have the left/the peace movement/the social movements—call it or them what you will—barked up the wrong tree? Should we instead urge the US towards the sort of global role urged on it by its neoconservatives (some of them former leftists) who have steered the foreign policy of the George W. Bush administration? My answer is, unsurprisingly, no; but why we should say no to such an historical adventure deserves a deeper grounding than we have given it to date.

The first thing to say is that the usual arguments against supporting policies of unilateral military intervention or invasion are not sufficient. Such military interventions have been argued against for centuries on the principle of the Westphalia system, developed at the conclusion of the Thirty Years War, and designed to ensure that Europe did not tear itself apart along the contours of religious and ethnic difference. The nation-state became the stable unit of international citizenship, with conduct within its borders of legitimate concern to other states only insofar as it affected their well-being— for example, the massing of armies behind the border. The policy did not even pretend to be a moral one. Untold atrocities could occur over the other side of the fence—and might even be welcomed, as they would weaken the enemy—and nothing was demanded of neighbouring nations.

This position is still the one taken by American conservatives (non neo-), grouped around publications like the *American Conservative*, and also of maverick Tories such as Peter Hitchens, brother of Christopher and a holder of—to put it politely—idiosyncratic views (he called the war a 'socialist' one). That the Westphalia system is inadequate in the face of modern technology has been oft-noted since the development of the bomber-aeroplane in the 1920s; and it was coincident with that development that all major states acquired intelligence and espionage services. The invention of missiles and weapons of mass destruction has further complicated the rational application of the system, but these weapons have not made it useless—they have simply made it absolutely essential that the relationship between a government and its intelligence services be as transparent and proper as possible.

Yet the Westphalia system has always been based on a realpolitik recognition of any national administration which can secure its own borders and prevent those under its rule from attacking other states, and which can be negotiated with. That the form of the nation-state—its ethnic composition and rulers—is often a matter of pure circumstance and good or bad luck, is not only not an impediment to the Westphalia process, it is central to it. Hitherto, this principle has governed a number of US overseas interventions—most notably in Somalia, where the aim was simply to establish a preferred set of warlords as governors. The fact that states arise from historical contingency, and frequently involve the suppression of one ethnicity by another, is sufficient to render the Westphalia principle itself a highly compromised guide to action for anyone who believes in the moral right to armed revolt against oppression.

Thus we cannot fall back on the Westphalia system—as many have done, particularly in the international law movement—as a necessary and sufficient ground for deciding which invasions to support and which to contest. Nor, historically, has the left done so. Nor, at the other extreme, can it support absolute pacifism, if it wishes to preserve, as it must, the moral right to armed revolt. Of course, very few of those in the anti-war movement were pacifist; many overwhelmingly supported intervention in East Timor in 1999, and the charge of pacifism is one of the most wilfully inaccurate criticisms that supporters of the war have bandied about. A more popular position, often confused with pacifism, is that taken by the various internationalist Marxist groups which is to refuse support to any military action by capitalist states, on the grounds that their state apparatus is an agent of class interests, even in the most seemingly humanitarian circumstances.

A third position is to regard military interventions as strategic events in the unfolding of historical developments that will advance states from dictatorship to bourgeois parliamentary regimes, and create a context for the development of a socialist movement and revolution. This is the position taken by Marxists who have historically shown more interest in co-operating with nationalist movements—in particular Maoists, some of whom have actively supported US intervention as a motive force in history.

Thus the spectrum becomes immensely complicated—figures on the right of the labour movement, such as Mark Latham, summon up a deliberately crude anti-Americanism (or opposition to the US alliance), while figures from the far left accept the arguments of the US neoconservatives in their claim to be continuing the American revolution.

Politically, the 'strategic' relationship to military interventions is attractive, and it is certainly the one to which the left has subscribed most frequently in the past. But for reasons that are both particular to our historical era, and also derive from a critical analysis of such 'strategic' politics, it is a position that I believe can no longer be usefully or morally held. We are no longer on the eve of a global revolution, and the left can no longer regard international relations as simply the politicking of capitalist states. Nor can it ignore the moral and political disasters which a 'strategic' attitude has brought about in the past. Today, the onus is on the left to be the bearer of a well-reasoned, moral and practical philosophy of military intervention which can be consistently argued from well-understood principles. This cannot be a philosophy 'taken off the rack', of course, nor could one presume that it would be of indefinite or easy application. But nor is it possible to consent to the dishonest, opportunist, ungrounded and ultimately cynical policy of military humanitarianism in place today.

The key political and historical factor in the character of the new era is of course the development of weapons of mass destruction, and the concentration of them in the hands of a single national power, the US. In the abstract we can say that the most prominent feature of such weapons is that they threaten omnicide—the total annihilation of humanity. In practice, the US is the only power with an arsenal sufficient to achieve this, though such an event could be caused by attacks by a range of other states with WMDs. These states— China is the most important—will eventually have an omnicidal capacity; at the moment they could kill billions, destroy whole megacultures (such as Indian or European culture) and render large parts of the earth uninhabitable. Further down the line, smaller states have arsenals sufficient to trigger larger wars—up to an omnicidal level—and a range of deterritorialised power groups, such as terrorist organisations or cults, will acquire or already have acquired them. Prior to the development of WMD arsenals, state power—even of the largest, imperial states—could be thought of as contestable within the array of global forces (that is, capitalism versus socialism, first world versus third world, and so on).

With the development of these weapons, the possibility of a catastrophic event arising from what had hitherto been the business of international relations—bluff and counter-bluff, a show of force, provocative action and pseudo-retreat—becomes immediate. In other words, the capacity of WMDs to undermine radically the conditions of life on the planet means that there must be—or be argued for—a radical shift in our attitude to and practice of conducting international affairs. The task of primary importance is to move towards a 'multilateral' situation—although 'multilateral' does not accurately describe the new principle—in which the control of such weapons is managed by representatives of the whole of humanity, out of an understanding of the way in which the whole of humanity is threatened by such weapons.

Thus the development of WMDs makes possible a new step in humanity's understanding of itself as having universal and common interests. On the other hand, a misunderstanding of WMDs that does not accept this entirely new aspect of their character, and which interprets them as simply very much bigger bombs, is the one most likely to lead to disaster.

The US represents the greatest threat to global peace and survival in this respect, not only because of the size of its arsenal, but because it is the state most liable to regard WMDs as simply 'much bigger bombs'. In the months before the war began, Defense Secretary Donald Rumsfeld made the historically significant but barely noticed remark that the US would not make a categorical distinction between nuclear and conventional weapons, and would consider the use of tactical mini-nukes for 'bunker-busting' operations. This, combined with the Bush administration's effective rejection of the authority of the UN Security Council, and the rejection of other international bodies such as the International Criminal Court, has set the US on a course away from any global or universal control of such weapons.

The refusal to acknowledge the radically different character of WMDs, and the desire to protect one's own arsenal, issues in a further development: the identification of 'rogue states' (and 'failed states', rogue states in larval form). Such rogues—the term originally means 'unherded animals'—gain their status by having alleged terrorist links, or by subscribing to an aggressive and expansionist ideology, or by being manifestly irrational. Some of these charges against 'axis of evil' states are valid, or plausible. Iran undoubtedly maintains links with terror groups (as of course do significant elements within the government of Saudi Arabia), and the North Korean leadership is embattled, and wrapped within a bizarre cult of Stalinist ancestor-worship.

Yet the imposition of a WMD-maintained world order by the US does not guarantee global safety, because there are any number of 'rational' courses of action that could lead to catastrophic human consequences. Morally speaking, the distinction between rational and irrational starts to break down when the weapons under consideration are WMDs. And the definition of a 'rogue' state can equally be applied to the US. It has armed potentially bellicose states such as Pakistan, for short-term political gain, and a significant number of its high officers subscribe to the particular form of Christian fundamentalism that places great emphasis on the imminent coming of the Apocalypse. Kim Jong-Il has undoubtedly directly presided over a more murderous and brutal regime than has US attorney general John Ashcroft, but it is entirely possible that the latter is no more 'rational' about the consequences of WMD proliferation and use than the North Korean leader.

Australia has less to fear directly from the 'rational' amoral use of WMDs by the US, but what of, say, the 'rational' use of WMDs by China? In order to minimise the risk both to ourselves and the whole of humanity, the only rational and moral course of action is to work towards a situation in which individual nation-states give up their

WMDs to some form of collective control. The policing of stray nukes, of terrorist groups with 'dirty' bombs and the like, would then fall under that purview.

This suggestion will seem hopelessly fantastical to many, in an era when the US has announced an unashamed policy of unilateralism and a commitment to spend whatever is necessary to maintain global military superiority. But it is offered as a goal, and possibly a state of affairs whose necessity will only become generally apparent after immense human suffering. Yet its supreme importance—by definition—subordinates other questions, especially that of humanitarian military intervention.

More importantly for many, it will seem to concede too much to multilateralism. After all, most of the arguments about the sham nature of much multilateral or global action are correct. The UN Security Council, up to its refusal to ratify the second US resolution presented to it on Iraq and WMDs, has been overwhelmingly a poodle of the US. Small nations in the non-permanent Security Council seats have been repeatedly threatened with denial of civilian and military aid. Israel is permitted to flout Security Council resolutions with impunity, and is protected by the US veto. Organisations such as the World Bank and the IMF implement US policy with regard to the extension of a global, borderless market. And so on.

All of this is true. One could even make the criticism

more general, and say that multilateral bodies composed of given entities—such as the UN, composed of nation-states—will always tend to protect the status quo, and will always deny representation to those whose interests challenge the manner in which the body is constituted. In the case of the UN, the exclusion of stateless peoples, refugees and so on from direct representation is likely to be maintained, because it is in the mutual interest of nation-states to do so. Yet what is being fought for in asserting the primacy of the UN is not the UN in its current form, but the principles of global consensus and dialogue in the safeguarding of the interests of humanity—principles which are contained in embryonic form in the UN. An analogy might be made with the British Parliament, which was characterised by pocket and rotten boroughs, a limited franchise and open and unpunished bribery for much of its early life. Yet it did evolve towards a genuinely representative system. The UN is overwhelmingly dominated by US and European interests, and subsequent forms would eventually be based on elements other than historically given nation-states. But it does have the capacity for a degree of countervailing power and the grounding of the principle of dialogue.

Furthermore, supporting the argument that military intervention in states should be ratified by a multilateral body does not necessarily imply that one has to end one's opposition to a war simply because that body has ratified it. In the same way that one can continue to protest and criticise a law ratified by a parliament whose general establishment one has supported, one can say: a) that the UN Security Council should be the ratifying body for any military intervention; and b) it would be wrong for the Security Council to ratify *this* intervention, and if it does we will continue to oppose it peacefully. There is no contradiction in that whatsoever.

Such a commitment to multilateralism and global responsibility must be argued for at a time when the relationship of trust between governments and people has withered to a significant degree, especially in the coalition of the willing. The lead-up to the Iraq war has seen the triumph of 'spin'—defined in this context as more than merely selling a position or statement; it is where the awareness of the importance of making a distinction between true and false statements as a precondition of moral and practical action has been lost. That the Saddam Hussein government was so murderous has been used as a justification for the outright lies told to people who were sending their sons and daughters to kill and to die.

Mastermind of the Iraq invasion Paul Wolfowitz recently argued that the 'weapons of mass destruction' issue was chosen as a *casus belli* because it was 'simple' and 'everyone could understand it'. It was also the only issue which presented Iraq as an actual threat to the countries from which the soldiers came, and it was also, as we now know, untrue and known to be untrue. Other supporters of the war, such as Pamela Bone in the *Age*, also minimised the importance of the existence of WMDs without apparent awareness of the inherent tension in their argument: that the establishment of parliamentary democracy and accountable government in Iraq was so important that presenting as fully factual as possible a case to the Australian people took second place.

What was already an overly consequentialist argument about how to make a moral decision regarding military intervention evolved into retrospective justification: because the casualty rate was 'low', the course of action had been right. Should the current turmoil in Iraq escalate to create a quagmire from which US forces have to be extracted, there will be large casualties followed by an Iraqi civil war and—quite possibly—another dictatorship. Will the triumphalist celebrants of the war further revise their opinion of it in that circumstance?

The question shows the absurdity of the *ad hoc* logic adopted by many of the pro-war party. For ultimately it is not simply what is done that one has to be judged on, but also what one was prepared to do. Given that the result of the war was never in doubt, the collapse of organised resistance by the Saddam Hussein regime was a mercy for the Iraqi people, even though a more hard-fought war might have prompted American doubts—and thus contributed to world peace. But Donald Rumsfeld and other members of the administration left us in no doubt that they were willing to contemplate an extremely bloody final phase of the war—and would rapidly switch from a selectively targeted bombing campaign in Baghdad to one far more devastating if necessary. And even an era of almost total 'smart' bombing did not spare several thousand Iraqi civilian casualties. True, a great deal of publicity and global concern was attached to such casualties, often to individual cases. But this had a malign side-effect—an utter disregard for military casualties.

There are times when such casualties have less import—those of an army launching an unprovoked attack, for example. But the Iraqi army were conscripts defending their homeland—whose humanity disappeared, apparently, as soon as they donned khaki. Nightly, on the news, the numbers of Iraqi military dead were racked up as if they were the score on a video game. Those troops who mounted an effective resistance against the US were labelled 'terrorists'.

The Iraq war marked a new phase in 'barbaric rationality'—an utter refusal to acknowledge the enemy's humanity. It was of a piece with the doublethink employed in mounting a case for war—that the 'truth' about Iraq was so important that lies had to be employed to sell it. That process has continued as the mass graves have been unearthed. There is no doubt that the Saddam Hussein regime murdered hundreds of thousands of people. There is no doubt that it continued to use execution and torture as a political tool.

But the bulk of the mass murders occurred in the period following the Gulf War, during and following the Shiite and Kurd uprisings, whose leaders had been promised US backing and airspace support. This was withdrawn once the Bush administration contemplated the prospect of an independent Kurdistan and an Iranian-aligned Shiite theocracy. The US actions do not lessen Saddam Hussein's culpability in the bloodbath that followed one iota, but they do constitute an odious and immoral betrayal, and one which, once again, can be sheeted home to the strategic, compromised and unprincipled doctrine of intervention. Between that time and this, and with the imposition of no-fly zones, the Saddam regime carried on political murders, but on nothing like the same scale. It is still arguable that the degree of day-to-day repression in Iraq was sufficient to warrant military intervention, but the case was never presented to the people of the US, the UK or Australia. It still hasn't been.

Under what circumstances, then, could military intervention be justified? Could we argue for a United Nations, with a differently constituted Security Council, which would have a mandate to make more robust interventions in places where governments or majority groups—ethnic or otherwise—are engaged in oppression and political killing? Yes, we could, as long as we are aware that such an arrangement still leaves unanswered the question of the criteria to be applied to the situations under consideration.

The left would want to be wary of encouraging the creation of a global force that goes beyond the purview of control of WMDs, and is charged with safeguarding or implementing liberal political order across the globe. This is not only because such political orders must be seen, in the last analysis, as cultural forms whose metacultural claims— claims to override other cultural forms—can never be validated. It is also because those societies which do fall outside the liberal framework may also be regimes which are, on balance, worth protecting. Castro's Cuba and Chavez's Venezuela are two examples.

The only circumstance in which one can derive a clear mandate for armed intervention (aside from a genuine invitation by groups or individuals who clearly represent a substantial majority of the population) is where a total, unconstrained genocide is threatened or underway. Contrary to what is often said, the distinction between ethnic violence which is not genocidal—an example might be Kosovo—and that which is leading up to it is usually relatively clear.

Elsewhere in this collection Raimond Gaita notes that genocide fulfils the condition where not to intervene would be to wrong the persons subject to the genocide. To come at it from the other end, one could say that, under circumstances of genocide, intervention is valid because there is no conceivable result of it that could be worse than the genocide that would result from non-intervention. There have been only two recent examples of this: the Vietnamese invasion of Khmer Rouge Kampuchea (Cambodia) in 1978, and the Rwandan genocide of 1994. In these circumstances, the multi- or unilateral nature of the intervention mattered less than that it be done. The Vietnamese toppling of Pol Pot was done for a mixture of reasons, most of them to do with border security. But it was also out of a recognition that something beyond even the most ruthless political calculus was occurring within Cambodia's borders. In Rwanda in 1994, multilateralism was used as a way of avoiding action. Put simply someone—anyone—with sufficient firepower should have jumped in and prevented the Hutu parties from destroying the Tutsis.

Under the schema I have suggested above, the left's role in that latter conflict should have been to urge intervention, at a time when no one was willing to think clearly about what was going on. At other times, however, it is to stand up for the principle of multilateral power, and beyond that, of humanity's collective control of the weapons that can eliminate our species. That will not only open us to the charge of acquiescence, it will test the mettle of those willing to advocate a principled policy for global security and peace.

But the century ahead is the valley of the shadow—humanity either gains control of the destructive forces it has developed, or we will cease to be. Nothing could be more pressing; no political duty could be more clear.

HOWARD'S WARRIORS
Mark McKenna

Since the Iraq war 'ended' in late April 2003, Australians have heard much about their brave forces who, having returned from the front, have 'served their country' well. Most often these reminders have come from the conservative government that made the decision to commit our defence forces to war in Iraq amidst considerable political division.

Casting a political decision behind the patriotic veil of the word *country*, the government seems keen to forget that hundreds of thousands of Australians marched on the streets to oppose the war in Iraq. Until the outbreak of the war, the overwhelming majority of the electorate remained reluctant to endorse war without the sanction of the United Nations. The *country* was deeply divided over the war.

When political leaders cry *country*, invoking patriotism, they disguise political division and obscure one crucial distinction. My country is not my government.

On 22 April 2003, Prime Minister John Howard informed the Australian people there would be welcome-home parades for Australian Defence Force personnel retuning from Iraq. 'We will have public parades,' said

Howard, 'so that the Australian people in the traditional open-hearted fashion for which they are famous, will have an opportunity of saluting these people.'

In Britain and the US, the idea of welcome-home parades at this stage of the war would have seemed grotesque. Coalition soldiers were still dying. The long-term outcome of the war remained unclear. Weapons of mass destruction, the justification for the war, had not yet been found in Iraq. The humanitarian crisis in Iraq, while not as dire as predicted, was nonetheless severe. Somewhere between six and seven thousand Iraqi civilians, we heard, had died in the war. Hospitals throughout the country were struggling to cope. Newspaper reports continued to carry stories of poor electricity and water supplies, disease, civil unrest and the emergence of well-organised guerrilla resistance to the invasion. Whatever the evils of Saddam Hussein's regime, the 'liberated' people of Iraq were enduring considerable suffering.

War was not over—it had simply been looking for a new language and was now depicted conveniently as a series of 'substantial skirmishes'. George W. Bush and Tony Blair continued to fight an intense political battle to justify the war. Meanwhile, in Australia, John Howard planned his parades for homecoming forces, those Australians that a Queensland talkback radio host described ecstatically as 'Howard's warriors'.

While the parades would be organised by the defence

force, they were clearly John Howard's initiative. Under-standing why he insisted on the parades, their recent appearance in Australia's political culture and their ultimate political purpose, offers a powerful insight into the way in which John Howard has changed both the office of prime minister and the Australian nation since his election in 1996.

More than any other prime minister in the post-war era, Howard has sought to gain political advantage by wrapping himself in khaki. Howard, the arch-constitutional monarchist, has succeeded in making the office of prime minister more presidential. Far from 'protecting the current system', he has Americanised the role of the prime minister in Australia. He is also the prime minister who, more than any of his predecessors, with the possible exception of Billy

Canberra Times, 19 June 2003   Courtesy of Geoff Pryor

Hughes, sees the most profound expression of Australian identity in military endeavour.[1]

Welcome Home

Farewell and homecoming parades for Australian military forces are not a new phenomenon. They occurred at the time of the First World War and the Second World War, but were not exploited by the Commonwealth government. As early as 1885, the streets of Sydney were festooned with streamers and imperial flags. As soldiers leaving to fight for the British in Sudan marched along Oxford Street towards Hyde Park, women ran from the crowd to plant kisses on their cheeks. The public theatre of the Anzac tradition is built on the parade of veterans through our streets every 25 April—our most emotional civic ritual. The call of the bugle at dawn. The sight of men and women of all ages marching proudly, the drums of the military band, the

---

1   On the ongoing presence and cost of US troops in Iraq see the *Sydney Morning Herald* 11 July 2003 p. 9. Alan Ramsey's column in the *SMH* 27 May 2000 p. 49 is valuable for its detail on Hawke and the Gulf War and Howard and Timor. On Howard's presence at a welcome for RAAF personnel, Tindale Air Force Base, see the *Australian* 16 May 2003 p.1. Howard announces his intention to have the parades, *Commonwealth of Australia, Parliamentary Debates*, House of Representatives Hansard 13 May 2003, p. 13962. Also see the *SMH* 23 April 2003 p.10—Howard speaks of the parades.

medals of the old diggers jangling on their breast as they pass by.

Military parades are as old as human civilisation and no stranger to the politics of recent years. In 1982, after victory in the Falklands War, the British prime minister Margaret Thatcher provoked considerable political controversy when she broke with protocol and took a march-past of returning troops from a platform outside the Mansion House in London.

In Australia, the recent welcome-home parades orchestrated by Prime Minister John Howard for forces returning from Iraq are unique in one fundamental respect—the presence of the prime minister and his leading role in proceedings. Before Bob Hawke farewelled and welcomed home the Royal Australian Navy vessels involved in the 1990–91 Gulf War, the presence of Australian prime ministers at welcome-home parades was uncommon. The convention was that the Governor-General officiated. In June 1966, for example, Governor-General R. G. Casey took the royal salute when troops returning from Vietnam paraded in Sydney. Even when one thousand Australian troops returned from Somalia in May 1993, Prime Minister Paul Keating was not present at the welcome-home parade held in Townsville.

While Bob Hawke was the first, it is John Howard who has manipulated these farewells and welcome-homes like no previous prime minister. Howard has elevated the role of the prime minister to that of the leading and central figure in the proceedings—a role more befitting an executive-style President—the Commander-in-Chief.

Under Howard, farewell and welcome-home ceremonies for the defence forces take place more frequently than any other non-parliamentary function in which the prime minister is involved. The frequency of these ceremonies is not simply explained by the different global security environment post-September 11. Rather, it is Howard's response to this new environment that is at issue. Since Australia's commitment to lead the United Nations Interfet Force in East Timor in 1999, Howard has personally presided over at least thirty farewells and welcome-homes for Australia's defence forces. This includes a reception for the crew of HMAS *Stirling* at the naval base in Perth on 24 October 2001, where Howard claimed that Australians were 'proud' of the navy's role in repelling asylum-seekers from Australia's northern coastline. Wherever there is a cup of tea to be had with the military, John Howard is there, delivering the major address, being photographed with servicemen and women and their families and generally basking in the reflected glow of the diggers' glory.

The fact that Howard first mooted the idea of the welcome-home parades long before the troops returned is but one indication of their true political purpose. Addressing Federal Parliament on 13 May, and formally announcing his intention to hold the parades, Howard emphasised that the war was 'just, legal and right' and that it had led to 'the liberation of the people of Iraq'. The parades were the first means of allowing him to shift his rhetoric away from the pre-war focus on weapons of mass destruction and chemical and biological weapons to the theme of the 'liberation of a sorely oppressed people'. A war that had begun as an American-led 'war on terror' in order to protect the world from lethal weapons became conveniently, after the event, a humanitarian crusade. Addressing a welcome-home ceremony at the RAAF Base in Townsville on 22 May, Howard told the assembled defence force personnel: 'You went abroad in our name in a just cause, and you joined others in liberating an oppressed people…you were not only great war fighters but you were great peacemakers and you were great conciliators.'

This statement differed markedly from Howard's comments made when farewelling HMAS *Kanimbla* on 23 January at Garden Island in Sydney, just as they differed from his address to Parliament on 18 March, in which he outlined the case for war. In this speech, humanitarian considerations were ranked eighth in the list of factors justifying war against Iraq. 'Liberation' was a mere addendum. Farewelling HMAS *Kanimbla*, Howard spoke of the need to 'disarm' a 'rogue state' in possession of 'weapons of mass destruction'.

After 22 May, the lie that the coalition of the willing had gone to war to liberate the people of Iraq would be repeated *ad nauseam* by Howard. The parades became a vehicle for allowing him to rewrite the history of the government's reasons for going to war, at the same time helping to cement the image of the war in the public mind as the successful venture of a benevolent government.

On the morning of 18 June, the day the first welcome-home parade took place in Sydney, Tony Abbott, Minister for Employment and Workplace Relations, addressed Federal Parliament. Without a trace of irony, Abbott told the house that it was necessary to 'suspend politics' (question time) so that 'the whole focus of our nation should be on welcoming home the men and women of the Australian armed forces'.

Far from suspending politics, the parades were a function of politics. Howard made it clear that 'the marches [would] be similar to Anzac Day marches'. For him, troops returning victorious from the battlefield of war seemed to occupy the same cultural space as Australia's sporting heroes. Explaining his decision to hold parades for the Interfet force returning from East Timor in 2000, Howard told talkback radio host Liam Bartlett: 'If we can have a parade for our victorious cricket team, our victorious rugby team, our other sportsmen and women it would be a strange country indeed that couldn't give a welcome-home parade to the men and women who were in East Timor.'

A strange country indeed. In Australia, national confidence comes through performing well on the 'world stage'.

Winners are winners, regardless of whether they win in war or cricket.[2]

The Legacy of Vietnam

One of the most interesting aspects of Howard's motivation for holding the welcome-home parades for both the Interfet forces and those returning from Iraq relates to the legacy of Vietnam. When explaining his reasons for holding the parades, Howard has repeatedly stressed that they signal a departure from the experience of the soldiers retuning from the Vietnam War in the late 1960s. In several radio and tele-vision interviews given in May and June 2003, Howard claimed that Australia had made a 'mistake as a nation thirty or more years ago', by not having a 'proper welcome-home' for the troops who served in Vietnam. The troops, said

---

2   Nearly all of John Howard's speeches and interviews referred to in this article are available on the prime minister's website (http://www.pm.gov.au/news/speeches/index.cfm). Howard leaves no doubt as to the government's motivation for war in his address to Parliament, 18 March 2003. For the theme of liberation see especially House of Representatives Hansard 14 May 2003, p. 14418. Also Howard's Anzac Day address 2003 and his address to the Liberal Party National Convention 8 June 2003. Commonwealth Parliament, House of Representatives Hansard 18 June 2003, p. 16767, Abbott 'suspends politics' and Howard 17 June 2003, p. 16577 claims the parades will be similar to Anzac Day marches.

Howard, had been 'very badly treated' by the political leaders of the day. This would not happen, he said, 'on my watch'. One interview he gave to Alan Jones on 22 May gives the best impression of Howard's views on the Vietnam legacy as a motivating factor for holding the parades:

> Howard: My sense is that the Australian public want to welcome these people back. I know that there is still a legitimate business [*sic*] entertained by people of the Vietnam generation who were almost secreted back under the cover of darkness. Now that is something to the great shame of everybody.
>
> Jones: It was a disgrace, wasn't it?
>
> Howard: Whoever was responsible for that, it was a disgrace. And I was determined when we made the East Timor commitment that when our troops came back, they would be given a public welcome, and they were…and I want the same thing to happen [for the forces returning from Iraq].
>
> Jones: Good on you.

The view that Australia had not welcomed home troops returning from Vietnam was also reflected in media reports of the welcome-home parade in Sydney on 18 June. The *Canberra Times,* for example, claimed that 'there were no comparisons with Vietnam as huge crowds waving Australian flags and green and gold ribbons packed into Sydney's CBD'. Interviewing Howard one week before the parade, talkback host Neil Mitchell saw the parades as a way of 'trying to avoid the Vietnam syndrome'. Servicemen and women involved in the Sydney parade were quoted as saying that they were worried they 'would come back and be treated like the Vietnam veterans'.

Within the coalition especially, the need to redress the treatment of Vietnam veterans was evident as early as 1987. Tim Fischer, Shadow Minister, National Party member and himself a Vietnam veteran, called on Federal Parliament to support a welcome-home parade for Vietnam veterans to be held in Sydney on 3 October 1987. The parade, organised by the Vietnam Veterans Association, followed closely on the heels of a similar parade for American Vietnam veterans held in Chicago in June 1986. In Parliament Fischer, reflecting the rhetoric of the Veterans Association, attempted to both vindicate and sanitise the role of the soldier in Vietnam:

> Vietnam veterans are finally to be welcomed home…Australian troops in Vietnam were not into drugs, even if they were into alcohol on occasions—I suppose that is part of our fighting tradition. They were not into civilian massacres and mayhem…the house might allow me to say: We went, we served and we are glad that we are going to be welcomed home at last.

Sixteen years later, after Australia's forces returned from Iraq, regardless of who was speaking—Prime Minister John Howard, journalists, or defence force personnel—the belief that was peddled by Fischer in 1987 still ran deep. Soldiers returning home from Vietnam had been treated appallingly and had not been welcomed home. This was but one memory the parades in 2003 were meant to bury. There was, however, one crucial problem with this belief. It was not true.

In Sydney in June 1966 thousands of people lined the streets to welcome home the First Battalion of the Royal Australian Regiment from Vietnam. The parade was televised live on the ABC. One protester, a woman, ran from the crowd and tried to smear soldiers with red paint, an action that, as Peter Cochrane has written, was at odds with the sentiment of the crowd. Contrary to the impression fostered by the vocal 1960s counter-culture, the Vietnam War, for most of its duration, was a popular war. In Brisbane in November 1970 tens of thousands of enthusiastic supporters welcomed home the Eighth Battalion of the Royal Australian Regiment. Between 1966 and 1970 there were more than sixteen welcome-home parades for soldiers returning from Vietnam, all of them attracting thousands of cheering onlookers. But how and why did the myth of Vietnam veterans as victims of a hostile home-front come to be so widespread and to be adopted so enthusiastically by the likes of John Howard in the aftermath of the Iraq war? Historians of the Vietnam War offer some answers.

Jane Ross has pointed out that 'from the time of the formation of the Vietnam Veterans Association in 1980, it was successful in defining the public image of the Vietnam Veteran as an overwhelmingly negative one'. Betraying a touch of amnesia in relation to the parades held in the late 1960s and early 1970s, General Peter Cosgrove made much the same point from a different perspective in 2000. Cosgrove noted that the Vietnam Veterans Association had created a 'sea change' in the public's attitude to the Vietnam veterans since the 'belated' welcome-home parade in 1987.

The parades held in the late 1960s have been erased from public memory. But what has not been forgotten is the public memory of opposition to the Vietnam War and the fact that the US and her allies (Australia, New Zealand, South Korea and Thailand) lost the war. Public enthusiasm waned as the war dragged on and when it ended it left behind a bitter taste. In the following years the popular memory of the war was dominated by the anti-war movement.

Recent claims that the Vietnam veterans had never been properly welcomed home are in fact a plea to put aside the memory of social division that surrounded the war. It is this memory that Vietnam veterans have seen as the major obstacle to their heroic status in the Anzac pantheon. During the allegedly 'belated' welcome-home parade for Vietnam veterans in 1987, many veterans refused to give eyes right to Prime Minister Bob Hawke (Hawke was present but did not speak), an action that reflected the veterans' ongoing bitterness over Labor's opposition to the war.

In 1992, when Vietnam veterans led the Anzac Day parade, this was perceived by many as the 'first' occasion. Yet Vietnam veterans had led Anzac Day parades in the 1970s. Jeff Grey, who has written widely on Vietnam, has remarked that the status of Australia's Vietnam veterans as genuine Anzacs has been 'made contingent on the way the nation had come to view the history of its engagement in Vietnam'. But John Howard's recent reliance on the myth of the ill-treated Vietnam veteran suggests that this collective amnesia has now become useful in a broader political context.[3]

By propagating the fiction that the treatment of Vietnam

---

3   On the Vietnam myth see the *Canberra Times,* 19 June 2003 p. 5. Neil Mitchell interviews Howard 13 June 2003. Howard's interview with Paul Murray Radio 6PR Perth 16 May 2003. Kerri-Anne Kennerley's interview with Howard 20 May 2003. Tim Fischer in the House of Representatives Hansard 24 September 1987 p. 685–6. Welcome-home parade for troops returning from Vietnam in Brisbane *Courier-Mail*, 13 November 1970 p. 3. Also Peter Cochrane *Australians at War*, ABC Books, 2001, p. 219. *SMH* 5 October 1987 p. 4 Hawke attends parade for Vietnam veterans. *SMH* 21 August 2000 p.4 Cosgrove on Vietnam. On Vietnam see Jane Ross, 'Australia's Legacy. The Vietnam Years' in *Vietnam Remembered,* Greg Pemberton (ed.), Lansdowne, 1993 (1990) pp 186–213 and J. Doyle, J. Grey and Peter Pierce, *Australia's Vietnam War*, Texas A&M University Press, 2002; and Jeff Grey and Robert Doyle (eds) *Vietnam: War Myth and Memory*, Allen & Unwin, 1992.

veterans was a 'disgrace', Howard sets himself up (falsely) as the patriotic defender of Australian servicemen and women who 'put their lives on the line' to 'defend their country'. By blaming the political leaders of the late 1960s (conveniently left unnamed) for failing to honour returned soldiers, and implicitly suggesting that those who opposed the Vietnam war were also responsible, Howard made his message clear. Political and social division over the morality of war is at all times to be buried beneath the more important need for national unity achieved through flag-waving welcome-home parades for our troops. Peddling false history becomes a means of exerting control over the politics of war. Howard becomes the great redeemer of Australia's national honour at the same time as the war against Iraq becomes noble and just. Every welcome-home parade screened on national television carries this none-too-subtle message.

At the time of Vietnam, Howard, who had been elected President of the NSW Young Liberals in 1964, was visiting university campuses advocating support for the war. Howard has always resiled from the politics of the street—at least where protest is concerned. Today Howard's image of street protest, unlike that of many members of his cabinet (such as Peter Costello), is still set in the stereotype propagated in the 1960s to describe the Vietnam protesters. In Howard's words, protesters are a 'noisy' minority, 'the usual suspects', often falling captive to the leadership of the radical left. Interviewed by Neil Mitchell on Melbourne radio in February 2003, Howard claimed that the people who had taken to the streets to oppose the war in Iraq had spent 'most of their time attacking America'. Three days later, impugning their loyalty, he suggested the demonstrators had given 'encouragement to the leadership in Iraq'.

Howard's heartland is the silent mob, those who stay at home in 'the real world'. There, as Howard describes it, 'people are interested in how the economy is going, their jobs, their interest rates and those sorts of things'. In Howard's Australia, protesters, despite the fact that they are today drawn from a much wider cross-section of Australian society than they were during the Vietnam War, can never be said to express a main-stream view or to be reflective of a mandate for change. Public opinion, says Howard, is not 'measured by the number of people who turn up at demonstrations' and besides 'you don't demonstrate in favour of the status quo'. Except, that is, at welcome-home parades, where Howard has claimed that by 'turning out in their thousands the people were really speaking for the entire nation'.

Like the Anzac Day parade, the ethos of the welcome-home parades under Howard is entirely uncritical and deeply conservative. All wars become one. The distinction between the volunteer citizen soldier, the conscript and the profes-sional soldier is lost. Veterans from World War II and Vietnam join the crowds to cheer the marchers on. The specific political, legal and social context of each war is forgotten. What matters is not why we fought but *that* we fought. Performance, duty and sacrifice above all else—'Advance Australia Fair'.

Howard's parades, now so integral to Australia's national self-gratification and pride, became a means of eradicating criticism of the Iraq war, marginalising political opposition and drafting the country to vote for the diggers' mate—John Howard. The Labor Party, which can only scamper after Howard lest it be seen as unpatriotic, is left far behind. If you think this analysis is far-fetched consider the language and theatre of the parades that took place in June 2003 in Sydney and Perth.[4]

---

4   Howard on the politics of street protest, *SMH* 17 February 2003 p. 1. Howard on Greenpeace activists, *SMH* 23 April 2003. Howard interview with Kerri-Anne Kennerley, 20 May 2003, contains his comment on 'the real world'. Also Howard doorstop interview in Sydney 20 February: demonstrations have given 'encouragement to the leadership in Iraq' as they did all over the world. Howard interview ABC Radio in Townsville 7 May 2000 on the parades in Townsville and Sydney for the Interfet troops. More comments on street protests—see Howard 20 February 2003 interview with Jeremy Cordeaux Radio 5DN and interview on ABC 'Country Hour' 4 February 2000. Howard interview with Charles Wooley '60 Minutes' 16 February 2003; and 18 February 2003 interview on Channel Nine 'Today Show'. Howard on protesters, see his interview with Neil Mitchell, 21 February 2003: 'they spend most of their time attacking America'. Liberal Party Convention, 8 June 2003, Howard attacks Labor for its opposition to the war as a cave-in to the 'fanatical anti-American left of the Australian Labor Party'.

Hogging the limelight

In Sydney on 18 June 2003 and in Perth on 20 June, thousands of people lined the streets, many of them clutching Australian flags, waving, cheering and calling out 'good on you digger' as the servicemen and women marched by. Above them, RAAF F/A-18 fighter jets and Navy helicopters flew past. These images, screened nationwide, tap the vein of national pride like no other—a triumph of emotion over reason. They also show Howard addressing the adoring crowd, congratulating soldiers and sailors, embracing their wives and children—images worth an incalculable amount of political capital. The headlines and reports in the nation's press reflected a similar story—'Cheering Crowds Close Ranks behind Gulf Heroes', 'Stirring Welcome for Aussie War Heroes', 'A great day to be Australian'. As Hobart's *Mercury* put it, 'There were no anti-war protesters yesterday, just an emotional outpouring of patriotic support.'

The Murdoch press was little more than a propaganda arm of the war machine. Melbourne's *Herald Sun* had carried a logo on its front page since the Iraq War began—'We Support Our Troops'. Editorials written after the parades in papers such as the *Daily Telegraph* in Sydney trumpeted the war using the same words as the prime minister—'a just cause'. In Brisbane, the *Courier-Mail* was keen to stress that those on parade 'carried no weapons'. Reportage and photographic material of the parades was replicated in Murdoch papers throughout the country. Tasmanians, South Australians and Victorians read the same 'news' as people in New South Wales. The size of photographs and headlines was the only evidence of media diversity.

On commercial radio the story was little different with talkback radio hosts tripping over one another to ingratiate themselves with the prime minister and contribute to the patriotic fervour. In the same interview with Alan Jones in May in which Howard expressed his determination to hold welcome-home parades, caller after caller rang to congratulate him ('I don't have a question. I just want to say thank-you for being at the helm'; 'We couldn't have a better man at the job'). The only probing question concerned the legality of making the burning of the Australian flag a criminal offence. On the same day, Howard was interviewed by Steve Price on Radio 4TO FM in Townsville. The conversation reveals Howard's skill in using homecoming troops as a means of pushing criticism of the war aside.

> Price: Gidday, Boss. How are you, mate? Mate, the amount of time you've spent with our troops…it's a wonder you haven't been made an honorary private…Mate, when you talk to the families, like I notice when you wander around, we see it on the telly, you talk to the families too. What do the mums ask you?

Howard:…I did not find very many people who were critical of the decision. I mean a lot of people don't comment on it. They take the view—well, the governments are elected to take these decisions and we'll go along with the decision. Others were quite supportive of it…[and the families] are naturally happy that they're being properly welcomed home.

In the nation's parliaments and in the media few voices could be heard questioning the parades—either their timing, given that American and British soldiers were still being killed and the Iraqi people were still suffering—or their propriety, given that the government's rationale for war was beginning to look increasingly bogus. Instead, Australians seemed content to agree with General Peter Cosgrove who described the parades as 'a day of rejoicing'.

At times the language of both Cosgrove and Howard became chauvinistic. Howard described Perth as a city that 'bulked' in Australian's defence while Cosgrove, speaking later at a private reception following the Perth parade, suffered from more Rambo-like delusions, telling his audience that Perth and the state of Western Australia was 'the Australian Warrior's gateway'. The warrior image had already surfaced one month earlier in Howard's interview with Steve Price. After a welcome-home ceremony in Townsville, described by Price as 'a garrison city', Howard was presented with a gift from the defence forces. As Price put it, 'the boys gave you a spear from Howard's warriors'. This spear now has 'pride of place' in the prime minister's office in Canberra.

Howard's welcome-home parades were also an example of the manner in which the persona of the digger, a sacred figure of national worship, is now perceived as being detached from politics—the khaki monarch of the antipodes. One of the messages that was repeated constantly during the parades was that they were an occasion to put politics aside and 'show we care' for our troops.

Brigadier Maurie McNarn saw the ability to make the distinction between the politics of war and the troops themselves as a 'sign of the educational maturity of our society'. One mother of three who attended the parade in Sydney told a reporter from the *Sydney Morning Herald*, 'They're the Aussies, aren't they.' Others in the crowd claimed that the diggers, by going to Iraq, had gone to 'protect our country' and 'there's something wrong with this country if we can't show our appreciation'. Comments such as these reveal not so much the maturity of Australian political culture, but its utter determination to 'close ranks' behind 'the diggers'. Many people seem unable or unwilling to see that the cries of 'rally round the troops' are deeply political, smothering questions concerning the legality of the war in a sea of patriotism. Backbenchers with defence establishments in their electorates were among the first to be invited to attend the parades. Far from being a figure above politics, the parading digger is employed by John Howard and sections of the media to increase the popularity of the conservative government.

Howard's duplicity is clear. When Australian forces left for Iraq he insisted that they went not 'in the name of the government of the day', but 'in the name of Australia'. Speaking at welcome-home parades and ceremonies, however, Howard emphasised that he was 'the person who, more than anybody else in Australia, of course accepts responsibility for the decision to deploy you'. One moment the diggers are fighting for their country. The next moment they are being reminded that it is their prime minister who sends them to war. And it is precisely this moment when Howard seeks to receive personal credit and gain political advantage by identifying himself with the diggers on parade. On the rare occasion when Howard was challenged over his use of the parades, he appeared angry and stung, probably because it was such an unusual experience for him. On talkback radio in Perth, one caller, who claimed to be a Vietnam veteran, accused Howard of 'trying to use the defence forces for political gain by hogging the limelight'. Howard responded incredulously:

> He says I hog the limelight. Well, I'm the prime minister…I'm the person responsible. If I didn't turn up, just imagine if I didn't turn up at the parade and I said nothing—people would say, for heaven's above, he's the bloke who sent us, he hasn't

even come along to welcome us back. I mean, really, this is…a bit cheap.

Howard is certainly the prime minister, but the political expectations he describes are those of his own making. Howard is the prime minister who is ever keen to remind the electorate that 'he is the bloke' who sends the troops to war. Howard is the prime minister who has created the impression that the leading presence of the prime minister at welcome-home parades, and his role in instigating the parades, is necessary, desirable and natural. He has built the military stage on which the limelight shines.[5]

John Howard and the 'Australian military tradition'

Why is John Howard so drawn to the military stage? One clue lies in his personal background. Howard grew up in

5   Reports on parades: see *SMH* 19 June 2003 p. 1, *Herald Sun* 19 June, the *Mercury* 19 June p. 5, *Daily Telegraph* 19 June, Adelaide *Advertiser*, 19 June, *Canberra Times*, 19 June, *Courier-Mail*, 19 June, *Australian* 19 June, *West Australian*, 21 June 2003 p. 4–5. Alan Jones interview 22 May 2003; also see 13 June 2003, Howard's interview with Neil Mitchell who complains Melbourne can't have a parade of its own. 22 May 2003 Steve Price Radio 4TO FM Townsville. *Canberra Times* 19 June quotes Brigadier Maurie McNarn. Howard emphasises his personal role as the chief decision maker, see welcome at Holsworthy army barracks 20 May 2003. Also 22 May 2003 welcome-home Townsville RAAF Base and Howard's interview with Liam Bartlett 20 June 2003; 19 December 2002 welcome-home for final SASR contingent from Afghanistan Swanbourne Barracks WA. Also 21 September 1999, House of Representatives, Hansard.

Sydney's inner west in the 1940s and 1950s, in a suburban milieu that was uniformly Anglo, Protestant, deeply conservative and, in the words of Howard's brother, Bob, distinctly lacking in a 'critical intellectual environment'. David Marr and Gerard Henderson have both written perceptively on Howard's early years. Marr stresses the influence of 1950s Methodism in helping to produce Howard's sense of conviction and the 'unshakeable' 'moral foundation of his beliefs', especially values such as loyalty, sacrifice, obedience and the merit of individual achievement. Henderson draws out well the origin of Howard's deeply held faith in national unity, and his suspicion of plurality.

Unlike Fraser and Menzies, there is nothing patrician about Howard. More than many of his colleagues and Liberal predecessors, he has the common touch and believes wholeheartedly in the egalitarian myth, particularly when it is expressed through the figure of the ordinary soldier.

Reading the limited material available on Howard's early years, one image stayed in my mind—a comment made by Howard to Milton Cockburn in an interview for the *Sydney Morning Herald* in 1989. Ever conscious of the Churchillian heritage his father had bestowed on him with the name 'Winston', Howard told Cockburn of one of his strongest memories. He recalled 'standing on Ludgate Hill in drizzling rain, watching Winston Churchill's funeral procession and feeling proud to hear Bob Menzies give a speech which left the others for dead'. In the 1965 speech that so impressed Howard, Menzies described World War II as the 'great crucial moment in modern history', chiding the 'defeatists who felt that prudence required submission on such terms as might be had and others who thought that victory was impossible'. This was a time, said Menzies, when 'one man, with one soaring imagination, with one fire burning in him, and with one unrivalled capacity for conveying it to others, won a crucial victory…for the very spirit of human freedom'. Churchill, he said, was someone who spoke for 'the simple and enduring feelings of ordinary men and women'. Among the last lines of his speech were the words 'with one heart we all feel, with one mind we all acknowledge'.

Here, in Menzies' words, is the spirit of much of John Howard's political vision. The image of one people united, one shared common culture and heritage, the great virtue of the 'ordinary' person and, most importantly, the implicit understanding that it is only in times of national crisis and military conflict that the greatest prime ministers can emerge. On many occasions, Howard has stressed that his 'hardest', 'most emotional' and 'proudest' moments as prime minister have been connected with the commitment of Australia's forces abroad.

In 1998 Howard told David Marr, 'I am the bloke who ultimately wins the battle, and in political terms that is Churchill.' But Howard's identification with Churchill goes beyond the cliché of the dogged survivor. Churchill's most significant impact on Howard can be most easily seen in the area of foreign policy. More than any other politician in Federal Parliament, Howard is captive to the anti-appeasement mentality championed by Churchill. Launching the coalition's veterans' affairs policy before the 2001 election, Howard claimed that 'it was the refusal of free peoples and free men and women to recognise the nature of the challenge in the 1930s that brought about the terrible events...of World War II'. 'The principle,' he said, is 'the same' today. Many times throughout the Iraq war, Howard made similar analogies—'If you don't take a stand, dealing with it later on occurs at a much greater cost. That is what history tells us.' In this sense, Howard's determination to support America in Iraq is due to his long-standing belief in the historical benefits of military action over appeasement, as much as it is born of his willingness to uphold Australia's alliance with the US. But there are other aspects of Howard's belief in the culture and values of military service, grounded also in his early life, that have seen him remake Australian identity and the office he has held since 1996.

Judith Brett has written recently that Howard is 'astonishingly successful in linking Australian liberalism to the Australian legend', describing him as a leader 'fascinated by the lessons of war'. She is probably one of the first to understand what she terms Howard's 'takeover of the symbolic repertoire of Australia's radical nationalist past'. But there is still room to explain how Howard has achieved this 'takeover' and, by so doing, managed to claim much of Labor's traditional support base. The spear that holds pride of place in Howard's office is a good starting point.[6]

Reading Howard's speeches delivered before a military audience, I think it is possible to argue that his interest in war goes far beyond fascination. For John Howard PM, the most profound expression of Australian character is found in military endeavour. Speaking at a welcome-home morning tea for Brigadier Maurie McNarn and ADF personnel at Parliament House in June 2003, Howard spoke of his visit to Qatar where he met with the brigadier and his forces. There, he said, he was able 'to imbibe the sense of distinctive Australian-ness that clearly pervaded the operation'. The operation in Iraq was carried out in 'classically Australian style' by 'distinctively Australian forces' and 'a proudly distinctive

---

6   On the Australian military tradition, see Howard 19 September 1999 farewelling troops leaving for East Timor and again farewelling SAS troops 22 October 2001, Swanbourne Perth. Menzies' speech can be found in Menzies' Papers, National Library of Australia, MS 4936/6/219, BOX 282. Speeches etc. 1965. Milton Cockburn, 'What Makes Johnny Run', *SMH* 7 January 1989. Gerard Henderson *A Howard Government: Inside the Coalition,* HarperCollins, 1995. David Marr on Howard, *SMH* 4 July 1998. Also see Howard's interview on the Channel Nine 'Today Show', 16 February 2003. Judith Brett, *Australian Liberals and the Moral Middle Class: From Alfred Deakin to John Howard*, Cambridge University Press, 2003, pp. 202–06.

Australian unit'. They were 'part of a coalition operation, but always very Australian'.

On the occasion of Anzac Day parades and particularly since his decision to commit Australian forces to East Timor in 1999, Howard has spoken frequently of 'an Australian military tradition'. This 'tradition' is today one of the most abiding themes of his prime ministership. In almost every speech he delivers in a military context, Howard praises this 'great Australian tradition'. The welcome-home parades held in Sydney and Perth for Australian forces returning from Iraq were no different:

> You went abroad as part of a great Australian military tradition, a tradition that has never sought to oppress people, a tradition which has never sought to impose the will of this country or the collective will of a group of countries of which Australia is part, on other people and other nations, but rather a tradition that seeks to defend what is good in the world, that seeks to uphold the values for which this nation stands and seeks to deliver freedom from tyranny, from terror and oppression.

Howard's 'military tradition' is anti-military by definition, a tradition which asks Australians to be so naive as to accept that wars can be fought without the intention of imposing the will of one country, or a coalition of countries, upon another country. This peaceful tradition includes not only Australia's invading force in Iraq, but the SAS troops who boarded the *Tampa* in 2001, and the crew of HMAS *Manoora* who were responsible for assisting 'illegal' asylum-seekers to Nauru. All are linked inextricably to Anzac which, in Howard's eyes, is 'the great tradition born on 25 April 1915, one that has shaped the character and the destiny of this country more than any other tradition or influence'.

At the dawn service held in Gallipoli in 2000, Howard's minders distributed to the press photographs of his father and grandfather, both of whom had fought in World War I. In Howard's address on this occasion and in his address on Anzac Day in Canberra in 2001, he cast the Anzac tradition in the image of Australian liberalism. Howard described the Anzacs as having built 'a culture of proud self-reliance and personal initiative…a country where prosperity and opportunity are derived not by birth but by endeavour'. Howard's Anzacs are responsible for the birth of Australian democracy, free speech, and the entire Australian 'way of life'. In his 2001 Anzac Day address, Howard's language was evangelical:

> All over Australia, all over the world today, our countrymen and women are gathering—drawn together almost by instinct, by a great silent summons to repay a debt to the past. Each year the numbers of us grow. Each year, more and more young Australians hear the call.

For Howard, Anzac is an article of faith beyond rational or critical examination—a perennial spiritual pilgrimage that binds Australians together. Howard's religious zeal for Anzac is unique. In no other sphere of Australian culture or politics does he betray the same depth of feeling or employ such pious language. While he denies the importance of symbolism in areas such as reconciliation and the republic, he revels in the symbolism of Anzac. In Howard's speech at the welcome-home parade in Sydney in June 2003, he addressed the crowd as 'brothers and sisters, lovers and mates' as the 'great defence community family'. Speaking at an army centenary parade in 2001 he told soldiers, 'You are part of our identity, you are part of our language, you are part of our inheritance. Without you we would not be where we are today.' For John Howard, it is through the memory of war, and his personal leadership of military engagement as prime minister, that the nation finds its most meaningful expression. Australia becomes a community through the shared experience of war. Anzac is the soul of the nation, its single and most profound unifying belief. One which must never be challenged, criticised or condemned lest the nation lose its way.

More than any other Australian prime minister, Howard relishes the role of the chief storyteller in Anzac mythology. In this role, Howard speaks of 'joining the past with the present', a link he is keen to deny in other contexts such as the debate over the acknowledgment of frontier violence or the Stolen Generations. Although Anzac Day had already been resuscitated by the time Howard came to power in 1996, he has taken the legend to unassailable heights, a fact which has only further entrenched his political supremacy.[7]

President Howard?

With Howard's political supremacy has come considerable hubris and much greater symbolic power invested in the office of prime minister. At the Sydney parade for the forces returning from Iraq, Howard himself took the royal salute as he stood on a dais together with Sir Guy Green, Chief Administrator of the Commonwealth, and General Peter Cosgrove, the Chief of the Defence Force. Howard, of course, also delivered the major address. The long-standing convention is that the Governor-General alone should take the royal

---

7   On Anzac as the protector of democracy see Howard's address 'Defenders of Australia', 23 April 2002. 22 October 2001 Howard lumps the *Tampa*, the Timor commitment and the send-off of SAS troops to Afghanistan together. Similar example 13 October 2001, when Howard praises the crew of HMAS *Manoora* for taking illegal asylum-seekers to Nauru. Howard reflecting on his role in sending troops to war, National Congress of RSL address, 5 September 2001; opening of the ANZAC memorial at Gallipoli peninsula in 2000 and his interview with Mike Gibson, 25 February 1998. For Howard on joining 'the past with the present' see his speech at the launch of the Gallipoli 2000 campaign, 11 April 2000.

salute at homecoming parades, as R. G. Casey did at the Sydney welcome-home parade in 1968 and Sir William Deane did at the parade for Interfet forces in 2000. Howard's decision to take the royal salute at the Sydney parade is a break with protocol and an indication of his new role.

Under Howard, the conventional role of the Governor-General as the symbolic Commander-in-Chief and ceremonial figurehead has been usurped. This has been particularly noticeable at farewells and welcome-homes for military personnel since 1999. On the occasion of the farewell for HMAS *Kanimbla* in January 2003, the Governor-General, Dr Peter Hollingworth, was invited to attend but did not speak and played no formal ceremonial role.

Hollingworth's poor standing in the community is not of itself sufficient explanation. Howard had already shown a determination to usurp the role established by Governor-General Sir William Deane. In October 1999, at the opening of the Nurses Memorial in Canberra, Deane was relegated to the role of ribbon-cutter while Howard delivered the major address. When troops departed from Darwin for East Timor in 1999, Deane was not invited to attend. In Townsville in November 2002, Howard and Hollingworth were present at the opening of the revamped Air Force memorial. The report in the *Australian* the following day noted that the Governor-General had been 'left out in the cold' by Howard, a lone figure relegated to nodding approval of the prime minister's speech. Howard may claim to be a constitutional monarchist, but his vision of the vice-regal office is one which sees the Governor-General as little more than the noble puppet of a presidential prime minister.[8]

The Last Parade?

With the 'war' in Iraq now indexed under 'ongoing American presence', its long-term outcome remains unclear. Since the war began, many commentators have wondered why, in Australia, John Howard has escaped the negative political fallout suffered by Tony Blair and George Bush. Aside from the obvious reasons such as the absence of Australian casualties, our relatively small commitment, and its short duration, there are other reasons which are more difficult to discern.

Through Howard's exploitation of farewell and welcome-home parades for Australian forces returning from Iraq, and his manipulation of the Anzac tradition, he has

---

8   Opening of Nurses Memorial in Canberra, 2 October 1999. Howard's speech is on his website. *SMH* 19 April 2000 p. 12, Interfet parade. Revamp of Air Force Memorial, 1 November 2002. Hollingworth left 'out in the cold', see *Australian* 2 November 2002. Departure of HMAS *Kanimbla* 23 January 2003 see *Australian* 25–6 January 2003 p. 1. The fact that Howard took the royal salute at the Sydney parade (although not at the Perth parade where it was taken solely by Sir Guy Green) is confirmed by the record of proceedings held by the protocol section of the Department of the Prime Minister and Cabinet.

helped to create the impression that arguments over the war's justification are now a distant memory. Once the receptions and parades had taken place, the servicemen and women became Anzacs and, with this honour bestowed upon them, the likelihood of exacting criticism of the government's decision to go to war decreased. For Anzac has become a dangerous tradition in which critical debate and political controversy are whitewashed. Anzac engulfs dissent and division, burying any hint of disloyalty and deviance beneath the compulsion to be patriotic and stand by our troops. It has become the unifying tradition that John Howard has always imagined, a tradition which values blind allegiance and unthinking service more than rational and critical thought.

John Howard has often told Australians that the Anzac tradition reminds us 'not to fight new wars'. But this is only another scrap of Anzac mythology. There is peril in the relish with which Howard embraces his new-found role as the impresario of military parades. With each farewell and each welcome-home parade the ranks of the Anzacs grow. The march to war and the march home become natural, Australia's way of imagining itself as a nation, as the prime minister is so fond of reminding us. The more this theatrical display is repeated on our streets and in our media, the more war becomes accepted and peace the exception. This is what John Howard's beloved Anzac tradition may yet teach us.